Classic Math

History Topics for the Classroom

Art Johnson

Dale Seymour Publications

For my father, my first and surest inspiration.

Project Editor: Katarina Stenstedt

Production Coordinator: Claire Flaherty

Design Manager: Jeff Kelly

Text and Cover Design: Paula Shuhert

Illustrations and Composition: Publishing Support Services

ISBN 0-86651-690-5

Printed in the United States of America

8 9 10 12 13 14   06 05 04 03 02

1-800-321-3106
www.pearsonlearning.com

Classic Math

Contents

Introduction

Mathematics history is an essential part of every mathematics class, no matter what level. No subject is more diminished when deprived of its history than mathematics. The very nature of mathematics, with its own peculiar language and symbols, suggests a secret knowledge, open to only a few devotees. Nothing could be further from the truth, and presenting the developments of mathematical symbols, terms, and great thoughts will help students build a sense of mathematics as a living, breathing, and growing body of knowledge. Introducing the history of mathematics into a class serves to convince students of the humanity of the subject. In the minds of most students, math dropped down from the sky complete and correct. Most students believe that present-day mathematics has always existed and will always be. They have never conceived the idea that mathematicians made mistakes. Learning about history will help them change this mind-set.

Students see history happening before their eyes as they watch television news reports, hear new music on the radio, see obvious advances in technology when they use a VCR or a CD player, see new movies, and read new novels. Mathematics is different. To the casual observer, it may seem as if no advancement has been made since before Christ. This is simply not the case. As recently as the time of Shakespeare, an equation such as $4x^3 = 6x^2 + 2x + 3$ was written as "4 *cubus aequantor* 6 *quadratus* & 2 *res* & 3." Great questions such as how to prove Fermat's last theorem still baffle mathematicians and super-computers. In addition, the lives of some mathematicians are as colorful as any portrayed in a Hollywood movie. Mathematics knowledge grew by fits and starts, and was a long time in coming.

The goal of this text is to enable every mathematics class to benefit from mathematics history. It is divided into five distinct yet overlapping sections.

Some mathematicians appear in only one section, while others appear in every section.

Quote of the Week

A quote and background information about the quoter is provided to share with students on a weekly basis. Some quotations will lead to discussions of particular mathematics topics, and others will focus on the mathematicians who spoke them. The goal is to humanize mathematics for students. Emphasis on the roles played by women and men from different cultures will demonstrate the universal appeal of mathematics.

Event of the Week

The events selected involve people, situations, and events that shaped mathematics. Some events are of major mathematical importance, while others simply reveal a human side of the makers of mathematics. In the cases of Hypatia and others, where specific dates for given events are unknown, the mathematicians' entire biographies are highlighted.

Historical Problems

This section contains problems that are within the grasp of most students. Each problem is accompanied by some historical information for the student. The solutions, extension ideas, and additional information for the teacher begin on page 161. Although the problems stand on their own, many can be used to introduce new topics such as those highlighted in the extension ideas. For example, Fibonacci's rabbit problem can be used to introduce the golden rectangle, and the young Gauss's method of summing numbers can introduce summation formulas. In any case, these problems serve to present the human side to problem-solving throughout the ages.

History of Mathematical Symbols

Many of the basic symbols of mathematics, so familiar to all students, were developed under unusual circumstances. As recently as 1570 the equation $x^4 + 6x^3 = 20$ was written as $\overset{(4)}{1.}\ \overset{(3)}{\text{p.}}\ \overset{}{6.}$ *Eguale à 20* byItalian algebraist Raphael Bombelli (1526–1573). The origin of a symbol as simple as the plus sign leads to interesting conjectures. Besides the symbols themselves, the lives and events of the people involved make for interesting stories and discussions.

History of Mathematical Terms

Mathematics is a language all to itself, with its own symbols and vocabulary. Terms such as *isosceles, parabola, chord,* and *denominator* are strange-sounding and difficult to spell. All of them have a logical origin and, in many cases, an interesting background that will help students recall their meanings.

Including yet another topic in an already crowded syllabus can be a daunting task. The materials contained in this book are designed to humanize mathematics without requiring a great deal of class time. As vocabulary words and specific symbols arise in the course of the year, a brief discussion or comment can relate the history behind them. Once a week, a few minutes can be spent reading and discussing a Quote of the Week and an Event of the Week to reveal the human side of mathematics. This can be a "warm-up" activity at the start of class, as suggested in the 1990 NCTM *Yearbook.* Finally, the Historical Problems may be used to introduce a new topic, as enrichment activities, or as extra credit.

For students at all levels, the history of mathematics enlivens, enriches, and enhances the study of mathematics. Hopefully this book will make mathematics history matter as much to students as it does to teachers. As the great French mathematician Henri Poincaré said, "To foresee the future of mathematics, the true method is to study its history...."

1

Quote of the Week

When [in subtraction]
nothing is left over,
then write the little
circle so that the place
does not remain empty.

Al-Khwarizmi (al KWA riz mee)

Imagine you are the court astrologer for Caliph al-Wathiq, a Muslim leader, who has been stricken by a serious illness. He sends for you and asks you to predict whether or not he will recover. You suspect he will not. What would you do? That perplexing situation confronted Mohammed ibn-Musa al-Khwarizmi (c. A.D. 825), who was born in what is present-day Iran.

Al-Khwarizmi, one of the foremost Islamic mathematicians in history, is responsible for much of our algebra. The title of one of al-Khwarizmi's books gives us the word *algebra*, and a translation of his name is the source of the word *algorithm*.

Al-Khwarizmi introduced the positional numerical system of the Hindus, along with their ten numbers, to the world. He introduced the concept of zero (a little circle) in *The Book of Addition and Subtraction According to the Hindu Calculation*. Another one of his books, *The Book of Restoring and Balancing*, was the real starting point of the development of algebra for Islamic mathematicians.

Al-Khwarizmi also was involved in cartography (the production of maps). He wrote a book entitled *The Image of the Earth*, in which he produced a map of the then-known world that was an improvement on any such map drawn before, even the great map of Ptolemy.

In 1145 Robert of Chester, an archdeacon in northern Spain, produced the first Latin translation of many Arabic books, including the Koran and al-Khwarizmi's mathematics texts. Thus al-Khwarizmi's writings are the means by which the Western world gained knowledge of the concept of zero and the Hindu-Arabic number system.

What did al-Khwarizmi do about the caliph's request? Perhaps remembering what can happen to bearers of bad news, al-Khwarizmi predicted a full recovery. Although the caliph died ten days later, al-Khwarizmi's reputation was left unscathed.

Mathematics reveals its secrets only to those who approach it with pure love, for its own beauty.

Archimedes (are ka MEE dees)

How would you like to solve a problem whose solution is a number more than one-quarter of a mile long when written out? That is exactly the length of the solution to a problem posed by Archimedes (c. 287-212 B.C.) "out of love for mathematics."

Archimedes is ranked as one of the three greatest mathematicians in history. (Isaac Newton (1642–1727) and Carl Friedrich Gauss (1777–1855) are the other two.) He is best known for his practical application of mathematics to physics topics such as the lever and the displacement of water.

Archimedes also had a love of pure mathematics, epitomized by a problem called "The Oxen of the Sun," which some have attributed to him. This problem was included in a letter to Eratosthenes (a Greek astronomer) in Alexandria, to be solved "by those … who occupy themselves in such matters." Given the magnitude of the problem and its solution, it is possible that Archimedes presented the problem as an elaborate joke. The problem begins, "Compute, O friend, the host of the oxen of the sun, giving thy mind thereto if thou hast a share of wisdom. Compute the number that once grazed upon the plains of the Sicilian isle Trinacria [Sicily] and that were divided according to color into four herds, one milk-white, one black, one yellow, and one dappled." The problem goes on to establish the following relationships between the bulls and the cows, with A, B, C, and D referring to the different-colored bulls; and a, b, c, and d referring the the different-colored cows:

$$A = \tfrac{5}{6}B + C \qquad B = \tfrac{9}{20}D + C \qquad D = \tfrac{13}{42}A + C$$

$$a = \tfrac{57}{12}B \qquad b = \tfrac{9}{20}D \qquad c = \tfrac{13}{42}A \qquad d = \tfrac{9}{20}C$$

With only this information the problem has an infinite number of solutions, although the smallest solution is a total herd of 50,839,082. Archimedes added two additional conditions to the problem: the sum of A and B is a perfect square, and the sum of C and D is a triangular number. A triangular number is a number that may be represented as a triangular array of points, such as the following:

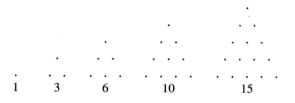

1	3	6	10	15

When solved with the aid of modern computers, the solution has 206,505 digits! No wonder Archimedes suggested this was a problem for those who occupy themselves with such things.

Give me a place to stand and I shall move the earth.

Archimedes (are ka MEE dees)

A king thinks he has been cheated. He has a crown that is supposed to be pure gold. It weighs as much as a crown of pure gold, but he suspects that there is some silver mixed in with the gold. He asks Archimedes (287–212 B.C.) to investigate. How would this greatest of all Greek mathematicians find the answer?

Archimedes is considered one of the greatest mathematicians who ever lived. He also discovered many principles of physics, such as the use of levers and pulleys. In this quote he presents the fact that with a place to stand and a lever long enough, he could indeed move the earth. He is also known for his discovery of the principle of water displacement.

In the story, King Hieron of Sicily approached Archimedes with the above problem. The king had commissioned a crown of pure gold from a goldsmith but suspected that the goldsmith had cheated him. The only known way to check on the content of the crown was to melt it down and compare the resulting lump of metal to an equal-weight lump of pure gold. If the lump which had been the crown was larger than the lump of pure gold, then the goldsmith had indeed cheated the king. If the lumps were of equal size, then the king would have destroyed his crown for no good reason.

Archimedes thought long and hard about the problem. It was while he was settling into his bath that the solution struck him. He jumped out of his bath, shouting *Eureka!* ("I have found it!").

Archimedes had discovered the principle of water displacement. If the crown were pure gold, then the crown and an equivalent weight of pure gold would both displace the same amount of water. When the test was run, the king's suspicions were confirmed: he had been cheated. The goldsmith paid the penalty due everyone who cheated his majesty, and Archimedes was handsomely rewarded.

I recognize the lion by his paw.

Johann Bernoulli
(ber NUL lee)

In 1696 there was a mathematics controversy raging throughout Europe. Who had invented the calculus, Gottfried Wilhelm von Leibniz (1646–1716) or Isaac Newton (1642–1727)? Both men had their staunch adherents. Leibniz published first, but Newton had dated notes which indicated he was first. (As it turns out, both men independently invented the calculus.) The controversy grew into one about the mathematical ability of each man. Who was the better mathematician, Leibniz or Newton?

In 1696 Leibniz and Johann Bernoulli (1667–1748) plotted to show Newton's weakness in mathematics. They circulated the following problem: What shape curve is the fastest route between two random points in a vertical plane, if the route is to follow the force of gravity? The curved route is now known as the "brachistochrone." For six months Europe was baffled.

On January 29, 1696, Newton arrived home after a full day supervising the workings of the mint to find the problem waiting for him. He ate a light supper and started to work. By midnight he had the answer to this problem and another one that accompanied it. He submitted his solution anonymously to the Royal Society, which forwarded it to Leibniz and Bernoulli. Although it was unsigned, when Bernoulli read the solution he had no doubt that it was from Newton, thus his quote about the lion and his paw.

Some years later, at the age of seventy-four, Newton repeated his performance with yet another problem submitted by Leibniz. Newton again solved a difficult problem after a hard day at the mint, proving he had no equal in his power of concentration on mathematics. In fact, it is said that he had no equal in all of history in his ability to concentrate all his powers on a problem, regardless of his fatigue or business of the day.

What did Newton think of these problems? He wrote to a friend "I do not love … to be dunned and teezed by forreigners about mathematical things [*sic*]."

From nothing I have
created another
entirely new world.

I have made such
wonderful discoveries
that I am myself
lost in astonishment.

Janos Bolyai (BO loy)

If you were challenged to a duel by thirteen different cavalry officers, how would you respond? Would you run, try to talk your way out of the fight, or try a bit of psychology? Janos Bolyai (1802–1860) tried some psychology.

Janos was born to a famous mathematician and professor, Wolfgang Bolyai (1775–1856), who tutored his son in mathematics. When Wolfgang became ill, he confidently entrusted his mathematics classes to his thirteen-year-old son, with no regrets or complaints. In 1816 Wolfgang wrote to an old college classmate, Carl Friedrich Gauss (1777–1855), to ask him to accept Janos as his mathematics apprentice. The letter went unanswered, and subsequently Janos attended the Imperial Engineering Academy in Vienna. He graduated in 1823 and took up a career in the army.

While in the army, Janos pursued an idea his father had unsuccessfully tried to deal with: the proof of Euclid's fifth postulate. The fifth postulate stated that through a point not on a line only one parallel may be drawn. Janos could not prove it either, but when he tried to deny the fifth postulate with the statement that through such a point not on a line, there are many parallels, he developed a "new world" of non-Euclidean geometry.

Janos eventually developed his findings into a twenty-four-page appendix, which was included in a book written by his father and published in 1832. The appendix has been called "the most extraordinary two dozen pages in the whole history of thought." Unfortunately, not many mathematicians paid attention, and Janos eventually learned that not only had Gauss had similar (though unpublished) thoughts decades earlier, but a Russian mathematician, Nicolai Lobachevsky (1793–1856), had published his non-Euclidean geometry in 1826. These events so devastated Janos that he never wrote about mathematics again.

What of the challenge by the thirteen cavalry officers? Janos agreed to duel them all, one at a time, if he could play his violin between duels. Whether the playing calmed Janos's nerves or frayed those of his opponents is not known, but the strategy worked. He won every duel. Shortly thereafter he was offered a promotion to captain if he would immediately retire with a captain's pension. Evidently, the army did not want to lose any more cavalry officers.

For God's sake, please give it up …it [the study of non-Euclidean geometry] may take up all your time, and deprive you of your health, peace of mind, and happiness in life.

Wolfgang Bolyai

The concern in a father's advice to his son is clear from these words. How could any mathematics topic be harmful to one's health? As it turns out, the father was correct. This mathematics was indeed harmful to his son's health.

Wolfgang Bolyai (1775–1856) was concerned for his son's welfare when he wrote these words. His son, Janos Bolyai (1802–1860), was trying to do what his father had not been able to do: prove Euclid's fifth postulate. For centuries mathematicians had wrestled with this postulate, trying to prove that through a point not on a given line there is but one parallel. All attempts were unsuccessful. Wolfgang Bolyai had once sent a "proof" to his college friend, the great mathematician Carl Friedrich Gauss (1777–1855), but Gauss found an error and returned his paper, along with some of Gauss's own work on the strategy of dealing with the fifth postulate by simply denying it.

Wolfgang's son, Janos, was involved with the fifth postulate from the start of his formal mathematics education, and as early as 1823 he was making progress in denying the fifth postulate and creating an entirely new geometry. Janos's non-Euclidean geometry stipulated more than one parallel though a point not on a line. He wrote to his father, "I am resolved to publish my work on parallels. All I can say is that I have created a strange new world." It took two years before Janos Bolyai could get all his ideas on paper and several more years before they were ready.

Janos Bolyai's ideas were included in an appendix to his father's book, *Tentamen Juventutem Studiosam in Elementa Matheseos Purae* ("An Attempt to Introduce Studious Youth to the Elements of Pure Mathematics"), published in 1832. Wolfgang sent a copy to his old college friend, Gauss. Gauss responded with, "To praise [this work] would amount to praising myself, for the entire content of the work … coincide almost exactly with my own meditations of the past thirty-five years."

Although Gauss praised the intellect behind the work, he never expressed such approval in print. The episode so devastated Janos Bolyai that he never published anything on mathematics again. A further blow came in 1840 when word of Russian mathematician Nicolai Lobachevsky's work on the same non-Euclidean geometry reached him. Worse yet, Lobachevsky had published before Bolyai had. This news sent Janos into a further depression, which lasted for the rest of his life. Bolyai's mental health also deteriorated to the point that he thought Lobachevsky's work was actually published by Gauss under a pseudonym.

The advancement
and perfection
of mathematics
are intimately
connected to the
prosperity of the
state.

Napoleon Bonaparte (bo na PART)

Napoleon Bonaparte (1769–1821) is known to nearly every student as a military genius and an Emperor of France. Few know that Napoleon was also an outstanding mathematics student.

He was born on the island of Corsica and while still a youth attended school at Brienne in France, where he was the top mathematics student. He studied algebra, trigonometry, and conics, but his favorite was geometry. After graduating from Brienne he was interviewed by Pierre Simon Laplace (1749–1827) for a position in the Paris Military School. While Napoleon was only average in other subjects, he excelled in mathematics and was admitted on the strength of his mathematics ability. He completed the curriculum, which took others two if not three years, in a single year. Subsequently, Napoleon was appointed to the mathematics section of the French National Institute.

As Napoleon rose through the ranks of the military, his ability in mathematics became well known, and mathematicians were drawn to this rising star. Italian mathematician Lorenzo Mascheroni (1750–1800) dedicated a mathematics text to him even before Napoleon became the ruler of France.

During the Egyptian military campaign of 1798–1799, Napoleon was accompanied by a group of educators, civil engineers, chemists, mineralogists, and mathematicians, including Gaspard Monge (1746–1818) and Joseph Fourier (1768–1830). On his return from Egypt, Napoleon led a successful coup d'etat and became head of France.

As emperor, he instituted a number of educational reforms and placed men such as Laplace, Monge, and Fourier in government positions with the commission to establish new educational institutions, recruit teachers, and revamp the curriculum to emphasize mathematics. Since that time, mathematics has been an essential part of education in France.

Lagrange is the lofty pyramid of the mathematical sciences.

Napoleon Bonaparte

Napoleon Bonaparte (1769–1821) is best known for his military successes and his empire. He was also an excellent mathematics student, and knew the implications of such a statement about Joseph Louis Lagrange (1736–1813), author of *Méchanique Analytique,* a text in which Lagrange proudly used only algebra and no geometric figures.

Napoleon was an average student in all subjects but mathematics, in which he excelled. He was the best mathematics student at his school in Brienne and was admitted to the Paris Military School by virtue of his mathematics ability. As his career began to rise, he continued his study of mathematics by keeping mathematicians in his company. A number of well-known mathematicians accompanied him on his Egyptian military campaign.

On return from the campaign, Napoleon assembled a group of mathematicians, including Lorenzo Mascheroni (1750–1800), Pierre Simon Laplace (1749–1827), and Joseph Louis Lagrange (1736–1813), to discuss mathematics. Napoleon was most proud of having solved one of Mascheroni's problems, the construction of a circle into fourths. As he began to explain his solution to the assembled mathematicians, Laplace commented, "We expect all things from you, General, except a lesson in geometry."

A theorem is named after Napoleon as well. He was not the first to discover it but apparently found it independently (although some dispute this claim), and so it bears his name.

In the diagram below, equilateral triangles are drawn off the sides of the given triangle *ABC,* and then the centroids are constructed. If the centroids are connected to form the vertices of a new triangle *XYZ,* then that resulting triangle is always equilateral.

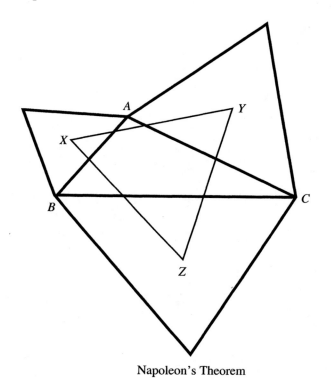

Napoleon's Theorem

Had Napoleon not become a great military commander, history books might discuss his mathematics, rather than his military exploits.

Algebra is generous; she often gives more than is asked of her.

Jean Le Rond d'Alembert (dah lum BEAR)

If you were abandoned at birth, adopted by another family, and now had the chance to meet your birth mother, would you do so? How would you react? This was the question faced by Jean Le Rond d'Alembert (1717–1783).

On November 16, 1717, a gendarme (French police officer) found a baby abandoned on the steps of the St. Jean Le Rond chapel near Notre Dame cathedral in Paris. A local glazier (someone who fits windows with glass) and his wife took in the baby and raised it as their own. The baby was named after the chapel where he was found. For unknown reasons, Jean added the name d'Alembert to Jean Le Rond when he reached adulthood.

As d'Alembert grew to manhood, he displayed great abilities in mathematics and literature. At the age of twenty-four he was admitted into the French Academy. Two years later d'Alembert published *Traité de Dynamique,* which dealt with the principles of kinetics and led to a fuller understanding of partial differential equations. Later works covered the mathematics of vibrating strings, wind, music, the motion of liquids, and the precession of the equinoxes. By 1754 he had been appointed permanent secretary of the French Academy. In later years he was a major contributor to the *Encyclopédie* of Denis Diderot (1713–1784).

After d'Alembert had become well known for his mathematics, his natural mother sent for him. She was Madame de Tencin, and his real father was General Destouches. Although the general abandoned his son at birth, he sent money to d'Alembert's adoptive parents and in his will provided a stipend that allowed d'Alembert to pursue a good education. D'Alembert's mother, on the other hand, had never contacted him or the glazier until d'Alembert became famous. She had not wished to hamper her social life with a child.

When he received word from his birth mother, d'Alembert visited her in order to tell her, "You are only my stepmother, the glazier's wife is my real mother." He never saw her again. For the rest of his life, d'Alembert lovingly cared for his adoptive parents.

When it is not in our power to follow what is true, we ought to follow what is most probable.

René Descartes (day CART)

What would you expect from a student who slept in every morning until eleven or twelve o'clock and attended class only when he felt like it? That was what French mathematician René Descartes (1596–1650) did as a student, a practice he carried over into his adult life. His habit of sleeping in was partly responsible for a great advance in mathematics.

Descartes was a sickly child from the very beginning. He was also a gifted student, and when he was enrolled at age eight in the Jesuit school of La Fléche, the teachers there were impressed with his abilities. They were also concerned about his weak constitution, so they allowed him to rest in bed each morning until he felt well enough to attend classes, a routine he continued for the rest of his life.

It was during one of these mornings in bed, so the story goes, when Descartes saw a fly walking across his bedroom ceiling. He began to think of a way to describe the geometric path of the fly in a purely algebraic way. The fly had awakened in Descartes the idea of analytical geometry, an idea that he revealed to the world in an appendix entitled *La Géométrie,* published in 1637 as part of his masterwork, *Discours de la Méthode.*

Would Descartes have developed analytical geometry anyway? Probably so, but the combination of a habit of sleeping in and the antics of the most famous fly in the history of mathematics brought the idea out even sooner.

I think, therefore I am.

René Descartes
(day CART)

Time and unforeseen occurrence play important roles in many people's lives, but few can point to a specific date and set of circumstances that turned his or her life in a new direction. For French mathematician René Descartes (1596–1650), there is a story that has such a turning point.

Descartes was born near Paris and received his schooling at La Fléche, an outstanding Jesuit school for the times. He was particularly good at mathematics, although he excelled in all subjects. At age eighteen he concluded that all learning was in error, with the exception of mathematics, which stood apart "on account of the certitude and evidence of the reasoning." In spite of this belief, Descartes pursued a law degree from the University of Poitiers and graduated at age twenty-two.

Upon receiving his degree, Descartes joined the army and was sent to Breda, Holland. According to one story, on November 1, 1618, Descartes' attention was caught by a crowd reading a posted notice. The notice was clearly a mathematical problem, but it was in Flemish, which Descartes could not read. He asked an older man in the crowd to translate. The man replied it was a difficult problem in mathematics, implying that it was certainly too difficult for a soldier like Descartes. However, Descartes insisted on the translation and upon hearing it, proclaimed the problem to be an easy one.

The older man replied that if it was so easy then Descartes should solve it, which he did in a few hours. Supposedly, the older man turned out to be Isaac Beeckman, the foremost Dutch mathematician at that time. Beeckman was so impressed with Descartes' natural talent in mathematics that he urged him to take up mathematics and give up his career as a soldier. When his tour of duty ended, Descartes did exactly that. Eventually, he invented analytical geometry.

What if the notice had been posted on a different corner, or in German? Suppose Beeckman had been late in joining the crowd, or Descartes had been on duty that day? Who knows? Coincidences are what make life full of surprises. This chance meeting changed the course of mathematics history.

Do not worry about your difficulties in mathematics.

I assure you mine are still greater.

Albert Einstein

Einstein

Albert Einstein (1879–1955) offers a study in the stereotype of the absent-minded professor. The many anecdotes about his life combined with his image of tousled hair and the complexity of his theory of relativity, produce a figure at once familiar and awe-inspiring. One such anecdote concerns Einstein's tour of the United States shortly after the publication of his paper on relativity.

The tour was a long one and took its toll on the young mathematician. One afternoon, as Einstein and his driver were headed to yet another lecture in yet another college lecture hall, Einstein had an idea. Speaking to his driver, Einstein said, "I really don't feel up to giving my lecture tonight. Why don't you deliver it?"

"Me?" gasped the shocked driver.

"Yes," replied Einstein. "You have heard me give it scores of times. I'm sure you must have it memorized by now."

"What if there are questions?" asked the driver.

"There are never any questions, are there? There is nothing to worry about," returned Einstein. And so the ruse was planned. They would change clothes and switch roles. On arriving at campus, the driver was accorded the welcome appropriate for a famous mathematician, and Einstein tagged along behind, as was suitable for a man of his station. The lecture went beautifully, as Einstein knew it would. The driver was actually better than Einstein, growing into the talk as it progressed.

At the end of the lecture the driver dutifully asked for questions. To the horror of both the driver and Einstein, a man stood up in the audience and asked a detailed question about an obscure point of the theory of relativity. The driver looked at Einstein with fear in his eyes but then regained his composure, began to smile, and looking directly at the gentlemen replied, "That question is a very simple one to answer." Then gesturing to Einstein, who was at the back of the hall dressed in his driver's garb, the driver continued. "In fact, that is such an easy question that I would like to invite my driver to the stage to answer it."

The truth of a
theory is in your
mind, not in
your eyes.

Albert Einstein

Einstein

Albert Einstein (1879–1955) is most famous for his theory of relativity. He developed much of the theory by doing "thought experiments" rather than by collecting data. He found the truth with his mind, not with his eyes. A Nobel Prize was awarded him in 1921—not for the theory of relativity, since too few members of the Nobel Prize committee could understand it, although they were convinced of its importance—for his discovery of the photoelectric effect.

The many anecdotes told about Einstein create the image of a kindly, forgetful scholar who seemed unexceptional. One story concerns Einstein's difficulty in finding his way home from his office at Princeton University. Einstein could get on the right street, but he was always trying to enter the wrong house. Finally, the neighbors came up with a solution. From then on Einstein didn't have to worry about finding the right house—he simply had to find the one with the fire-engine red front door.

Another story describes Einstein's relationship with a neighbor's young daughter. The girl's teacher noticed a great and sudden improvement in her mathematics work. When she asked the girl what was responsible for the improvement, the girl told her about an elderly neighbor who was helping her. The teacher told the mother, who approached the great mathematician at his home to apologize for her daughter. Einstein graciously explained that he looked forward to the girl's visits. "But it is such a waste of your time," said the mother. "What do you get out of it?" "Very simple," replied Einstein, "Every time I help her with her homework, she gives me a lollipop."

Einstein's kindly demeanor hid an acute, perceptive wit. When asked what the weapons of World War III would be, Einstein replied, "I do not know, but I do know what weapons will be used in World War IV. Sticks and stones."

Highness,
There is no
royal road to
geometry.

Euclid (YOU klid)
(to King Ptolemy I)

Every mathematics student has wished for an easy way to do mathematics! Even royalty is not immune to wanting a shortcut to success. Suppose you were the tutor of a king who asked for an easy way to solve a difficult problem. How would you answer? As Euclid's answer to King Ptolemy's request implies, there is no shortcut to mastering mathematics.

Euclid (c. 300 B.C.) is known for his book *The Elements,* which has undergone thousands of editions and has been translated into hundreds of languages. This book contains practically everything known, even today, about circles, points, lines, and solid shapes. As recently as 150 years ago, *The Elements* was still being read in its original language by high school students in England. The popularity of *The Elements* belies its lack of originality. It is unlikely that much of the book's contents originated with Euclid. However, it is Euclid's comprehensive categorizing and cataloging of others ideas that makes *The Elements* a masterpiece of geometry.

Euclid was a teacher at a school in Alexandria, where one of his pupils was King Ptolemy I. After Euclid finished explaining a long and difficult proof, the king asked if there was not an easier way to solve the problem. Euclid's reply has been preserved for our benefit today. Just as Euclid's masterpiece, *The Elements*, is still valid today, so is his advice to King Ptolemy I.

I have assuredly
found an admirable
proof of this
but the margin is
too narrow to
contain it.

Pierre de Fermat (fair MA)

No doubt Pierre de Fermat (1601–1665) could never have predicted that a personal note, written in the margin of a mathematics textbook, would be the source of mystery and discussion for nearly four hundred years. What was the proof referred to in this note written by the man who is called the "Prince of Amateurs"?

Fermat was a lawyer by profession and only dabbled in mathematics as a recreational hobby. But what a hobby! Fermat communicated with all the great mathematicians in Europe, disseminating ideas of various mathematicians, posing and solving problems, and inventing new mathematics such as analytical geometry and the probability theory. Another great mathematician, Bertrand Russell (1872–1970), said it was Fermat who invented the study of pure mathematics.

This particular quote refers to what has been called Fermat's last theorem. It was written in the margin of a book that Fermat was reading and discovered five years after his death by his son, Samuel. The book, a 1621 edition of the works of the Greek mathematician Diophantus (translated by Claude Bachets), contained the original Greek and a Latin translation of Diophantus' work on quadratic equations.

Fermat's note concerned an equation of the form $x^n + y^n = z^n$. It is easy to find equations with integer values for x, y, and z if the exponent n is either 1 or 2. For example $3^1 + 4^1 = 7^1$ and $3^2 + 4^2 = 5^2$. The equation with an exponent of 2 is an example of a Pythagorean triple. Fermat claimed to have discovered a proof that there are no other integer possibilities for this equation. That is, no other values for n can result in integer values for x, y, and z.

In 1908, Paul Wolfshehl, a little-known mathematics professor in Darmstadt, Germany, left a reward in his will of one hundred thousand German marks to the mathematician who could prove Fermat's last theorem. So far, there have been no takers. It has been proven that there are no integer values for all $n < 125,000$ and even for some values of n larger than that. In 1992 J.P. Buhler and Richard Crandall used super-computer technology to verfiy Fermat's last theorem for exponents as large as 4,000,000, although this does not constitute a proof. In June, 1993, Princeton mathematician Andrew Wiles unveiled what he believes to be a general proof of the type Fermat claimed to have found. However, Wiles' 200-page proof, which links Fermat's last theorem to elliptic curves, must withstand the scrutiny of the world's mathematics community before Wiles can claim Wolfshehl's prize and a place in mathematics history.

Did Fermat have a proof? It is hard to know. He was a very careful mathematician who rarely made an unfounded statement. He certainly was not bragging or deceiving anyone, since he never revealed his last theorem to anyone. This much is certainly true: generations of mathematicians have wished that Fermat's book of Diophantus' equations had contained a wider margin!

The deep study
of nature
is the most fruitful
source of
mathematical
discoveries.

Joseph Fourier (foo REAH)

Picture a man swathed in clothing and blankets in a room already stiflingly hot. Would you ever guess this man was a genius, a great mathematician? You would most likely wonder about his state of mind. Yet this man was the well-known French mathematician, Joseph Fourier (1768–1830).

Fourier was orphaned at age eight but was taken into a Benedictine school where he showed unusual promise, especially in mathematics. He was an ardent supporter of the French Revolution until its excesses revolted even him. During the early years of the revolution he was awarded a chair in mathematics at the École Polytechnique, where he was an accomplished teacher.

In 1798 Napoleon beckoned all manner of skilled men to join him on an expedition he claimed would free Egypt from the Middle Ages. Fourier jumped at the chance to go and remained in Egypt as a teacher until 1801, when the British took control of the area.

On his return to France, he began to work on his mathematical theories and continued to teach school. These were times of great change in France, and with each change in government Fourier pledged allegiance to the new leadership.

He even supported Napoleon in the brief period between his escape from Elba and his defeat at Waterloo.

In 1822 Fourier published his masterpiece, *Théorie Analytique de la Chaleur,* in which he presented the mathematics involved in the conduction of heat. The mathematics included what is now known as the Fourier series, a series of sines and cosines that can represent any function. The Fourier series is an essential part of modern electrical and acoustical engineering. As this quotation indicates, Fourier was an applied mathematician who took raw data, found mathematical relationships, and then verified his results with more raw data. This method was in contrast to the trend of the day, in which pure mathematicians developed theorems with elegant proofs to sustain their conclusions.

How did such a well-traveled, well-respected mathematician end up in a room that was hotter than the Sahara? It appears that when Fourier was in Egypt he concluded that desert heat was the key to a long life. Accordingly, as he approached old age, he decided to recreate the Sahara in his own house, so he wrapped himself in layers of clothing and blankets and stoked the fire to a blazing inferno. It didn't help. In spite of his blanket saunas, he died at the age of sixty-three.

Mathematics
is the pen
with which
God has written
the universe.

Galileo Galilei

Some mathematicians come to their craft by accident. Once there, however, they stay with mathematics in the face of all opposition. One such accidental mathematician was Galileo Galilei (1564–1642). How did Galileo come to study mathematics? As a university student he intended to study medicine, but after eavesdropping on a geometry lecture by Ostilio Ricci, a student of Tartaglia, Galileo began the study of mathematics and science. This decision was opposed by his family, since a physician would earn the equivalent of $1,250 per year, while a mathematician could expect only $65. In spite of their opposition and the financial consequences, Galileo stayed firm in his decision to study mathematics.

Galileo is well known for his many scientific and mathematical discoveries. This Italian mathematician-physicist-astronomer discovered moons around Jupiter and craters on Earth's moon with his improved model of the telescope. Galileo's interest in the telescope was not totally scientific. He knew merchants would pay a pretty price to know in advance of their competitors the origins of ships sailing into port.

Based on his findings with the telescope, Galileo concluded that the sun is the center of the Solar System. The publication of this theory resulted in Galileo's being branded a heretic (a church member who disagrees with the church's doctrine) by the Catholic Church. He also discovered that all bodies of mass fall at the same rate, in contrast to the prevailing theory by Aristotle, which proposed that heavier masses fall faster. It is said that Galileo demonstrated his discovery by dropping weights from the top of the leaning Tower of Pisa.

Galileo was more of a mathematical practitioner than a pure mathematician, laying the foundation for applied mathematics for subsequent generations of mathematicians.

Among the mathematical topics Galileo studied was a curve called the cycloid, which is formed by the path traced out by a point on a circle as the circle is rolled along a line. Galileo tried to calculate the area under the cycloid curve mathematically but could not. His practical bent was shown by his next strategy. He built a circle and its resulting cycloid out of wood and found the cycloid weighed nearly three times the weight of the circle. Galileo concluded that the area of the cycloid was thus a bit less than three times the area of the circle. (In 1634, French mathematician Gilles Personne de Roberval (1602–1675) proved the area of the cycloid is exactly three times the area of the circle that generates the curve.)

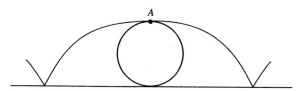

As the circle is rolled, point A *will fall on the curve.*

Galileo was one of the first to study infinite sets. He proposed that the set of counting numbers may be paired in a one-to-one correspondence with perfect squares, even though this seems to be impossible since the set of squares quickly reaches very large numbers. Galileo explained that since there is no end to either set of numbers, it is impossible to find a counting number that does not have a mate in the set of square numbers.

1	2	3	4	5	6	7	...
|	|	|	|	|	|	|	
1	4	9	16	25	36	49	...

Please remember me,
since fate did not
allow me a life
that would make
my name worthy
to be remembered
by my country.

Évariste Galois (ga LUWAH)

These words were written by Evariste Galois (1811–1832) on the evening before his death at age twenty in a duel with a professional soldier. Some accounts suggest the duel was over a woman, but the circumstances are unclear.

Galois was born the son of a small-town mayor and his wife, and displayed a great talent in mathematics from a young age. He was far superior to all the students at his local school, and to a great extent, was even better than his teachers. When Galois tried to enter the École Polytechnique, he had the bad luck to be examined by a professor of the school who had no appreciation for Galois's new mathematics of abstract algebra. No matter how Galois tried to explain himself, the professor could not follow his reasoning. Eventually, the interview and Galois's chances of entry ended when a frustrated Galois threw chalk and an eraser at the professor!

By the time he was seventeen years old, Galois had worked out the mathematics to determine the degree of equation necessary to have an algebraic solution. He delivered a copy of his paper to the prestigious Academy of Science for mathematician Augustin Louis Cauchy

(1789–1857) to read. Cauchy not only lost this paper, but also a second one which Galois submitted a week later. Galois submitted a newer, improved version of his work to the academy ten months later, this time sending the paper to the secretary, Joseph Fourier (1768–1830). Fourier died shortly after receiving it, and the paper was never found. One year later, Galois submitted still another revision of his paper to the academy. After a delay of six months, the reader of the paper announced that the paper's "arguments are not sufficiently clear nor developed enough," and refused to consider it for publication.

Galois was at his wits' end. Events conspired to prevent Galois from finding someone who would appreciate his work. He was dead within the year. His personal notes were eventually delivered to Joseph Liouville (1809–1882) who had them published by the Academy of Science in 1846, nearly seventeen years after Galois first submitted them. One can only wonder how Galois's life and the history of mathematics might have differed had Cauchy read that first paper Galois submitted.

I have the result,
but I do not yet know
how to get it.

Karl Friedrich Gauss (gowse)

Gauss

Two hundred years ago, mathematician Karl Friedrich Gauss (1777–1855) wanted to use mathematics to communicate with beings on the moon. This may seem strange, but it was just another idea from a man known for his flashes of insight. These insights made it possible for Gauss to see the result before he knew "how to get it" by working out the mathematics.

Gauss did not publish any of his findings until he had completely proven every aspect of his conjectures. For example, Gauss developed the beginnings of non-Euclidean geometry but wrote his conclusions only in his personal papers. Gauss's devotion to perfection is even apparent in his personal diary. Although this diary reflects nearly twenty years of his adult life, it contains only nineteen pages of entries.

Gauss was one of the last people to know everything there was to know about mathematics.

Since his time, mathematics has grown into so many varied branches that it is impossible for one person to be conversant in all of them. Gauss wrote about nearly every mathematical topic of his day, but he is best known for discovering and naming the fundamental Theorem of Algebra, which states that an equation of degree n will have n number of roots, thus $x^4 + 3x^3 - 4 = 0$ will have four roots since the highest power of x is 4.

Did Gauss ever communicate with beings on the moon? Gauss's desire to fully prove every conjecture did not keep him from indulging in a few flights of fancy. He proposed planting a forest of trees in the shape of a large 3-4-5 right triangle so that intelligent beings on the moon would see it and know there were intelligent beings on Earth!

Mathematics is the queen of the sciences.

Karl Friedrich Gauss (gowse)

Karl Friedrich Gauss (1777–1855) believed that mathematics is the essential focus of the sciences. He is considered one of the three greatest mathematicians who ever lived—Isaac Newton (1642–1727) and Archimedes (287–212 B.C.) are the other two. Gauss was like Newton and Archimedes in many ways. Like them, he had the ability to totally immerse himself in a problem until he solved it.

A story illustrates this rare talent of concentration. It is said that when Gauss's second wife, Minna, lay close to death, Gauss sought relief from his bedside vigil in the study of a mathematics problem. A servant called him to his wife's side, telling him that her death was imminent. Engrossed in his problem, Gauss looked up and responded, "Tell her to wait until I have finished here." Eventually, Gauss broke off his work and got to this wife's side, but his concentration in the face of such a situation is certainly remarkable.

Like Newton and Archimedes, Gauss was famous during his lifetime, even among military men. When the French army under Napoleon moved near Gauss's town of Brunswick, the emperor himself gave the command to spare Brunswick because "the foremost mathematician of all time lives there."

Finally, like Newton and Archimedes, Gauss was as accomplished in science as in mathematics. On January 1, 1801, a new planetoid, Ceres, was discovered. After viewing only nine degrees of its arc around the sun, astronomers lost it in the sun's glare. Astronomers throughout Europe searched for months to find it, but could not. Finally, some of the observation data was given to Gauss. He predicted where and when Ceres would be found. Later in the year Gauss was proved correct; Ceres appeared exactly where and when he predicted. This success moved Gauss into astronomy for the next twenty years, where he made additional discoveries by applying his considerable mathematical talents. He never left mathematics behind, but put it to good use in a field of science, as did Archimedes and Newton before him.

In mathematics there are no true controversies.

Karl Friedrich Gauss (gowse)

Gauss

What would you expect an eighteen-year diary to contain if its writer was one of the greatest mathematicians who ever lived and was known for his meticulous, methodical reasonings? The diary of Karl Friedrich Gauss (1777–1855), "The Prince of Mathematics," was only nineteen pages long, with but 146 entries!

Gauss made it a rule of life to record only those ideas which he had fully formed. He published even less than he put into his notes. He described all his life's work with a crest containing a fruit tree and the motto "Few, but ripe." What Gauss revealed to others was only a portion of what he had thought out. Those ideas Gauss did reveal were fully presented and left nothing more to be said. When he solved a problem he frequently ended the solution by saying, "Nothing further remains to be done." His revealed ideas were likewise complete, with no unfinished proofs or partial explanations. Gauss had ideas on everything, from non-Euclidean geometry to electricity, magnetic fields, astronomy, and much more.

Gauss's diary reveals how brief his personal notes were. The entry for July 10, 1796 contains the following cryptic message: EYPHKA!

(Eureka) num = $\Delta + \Delta + \Delta$. Essentially, this was Gauss's way of telling himself (he never published this discovery) that any integer may be written as the sum of at most three triangular numbers. A triangular number takes the form of an equilateral triangle when it is written as an array of dots. For example, 1, 3, 6, 10, and 15 are triangular numbers.

| 1 | 3 | 6 | 10 | 15 |

The equations $19 = 10 + 6 + 3$ and $42 = 21 + 15 + 6$ are examples of Gauss's discovery.

Gauss kept his diary for nearly eighteen years and then simply recorded his findings in a morass of notes and papers, some of which still await deciphering.

Algebra is but
written geometry,
and geometry is
but written algebra.

Sophie Germain

What parents would be unhappy with a teenager who did homework? What parents would forbid their teenage daughter to study mathematics in their home at night? It may be hard to believe, but that is precisely what the parents of Sophie Germain (1776–1831) did.

Germain was a mathematician who lived at a time when women were expected to stay home and leave higher education to the men. She had to overcome opposition from family and society to achieve fame and success in mathematics.

In Germain's case, severe opposition came from her parents, who were upset with her interest in books and especially her interest in mathematics. They discovered Germain was secretly studying in her bedroom at night, so they forbade her to bring a lamp to bed with her and made her go to bed in an unheated room without any blankets. They reasoned she could not possibly study her beloved mathematics in a dark, freezing room. They were wrong.

Early one morning the Germains entered their daughter's bedroom to find her fast asleep. She was sitting at her desk, pen in hand and wrapped in a quilt. There was a frozen inkwell at her side, her paper was full of calculations, and the candle she had smuggled into the room had burned itself out. From then on, she was allowed to study her mathematics in a heated room, with plenty of light and her parents' blessing.

Germain went on to gain the respect and assistance of two other famous mathematicians, Joseph Louis Lagrange (1736–1813) and Karl Friederich Gauss (1777–1855). She was awarded the grand prize by the Paris Academy of Sciences for her mathematical theory of elastic surfaces. She also created a theorem that was a major step in trying to prove "Fermat's last theorem." Eventually, Germain came to be known as one of France's greatest mathematicians.

Space and time are
intimately intertwined
and indissolubly
connected with
each other.

Sir William Rowan Hamilton

Hamilton

Imagine working for fifteen years on a new mathematics concept but not making a breakthrough until one evening when you are crossing a stone bridge over a canal. Suddenly the answer flashes into your mind, but you have no pencil or paper! What would you do? That situation confronted the great Irish mathematician, Sir William Rowan Hamilton (1805–1865).

Hamilton was born near Dublin to a wealthy family. His father was a lawyer. When William showed academic promise at a young age, his father sent him to live with an uncle who was a professor of languages. The uncle made Hamilton his private project, and by age ten Hamilton knew Latin, Greek, Hebrew, Sanskrit, Arabic, and a host of other languages. In his private moments, Hamilton taught himself mathematics. By his middle teens he had mastered all the mathematics commonly taught to students at public schools and could converse in over fifteen languages.

In 1823 he entered Trinity College with the highest grade on the entrance exam. Up to this point, Hamilton had never been to a school but had learned everything from his uncle and private studies. He was a brilliant student, predicted by some to be the next Newton. At age twenty-three he published *A Theory of Systems of Rays*, which dealt with the mathematics of optics. This revolutionized the study of optics the way Newton's work revolutionized the study of gravity.

In 1853 he published his greatest work, *Lectures on Quaternions*. Hamilton invented the word *quaternion* to refer to the algebra of solid rotations in three-dimensional space. Although Hamilton considered this to be as important a breakthrough as the invention of calculus, no other mathematicians shared his enthusiasm. Still, the concept of quaternions did open the door to over two hundred new algebraic structures. Later in his life, he was the first mathematician born outside of the United States to be elected to membership in the United States National Academy of Science.

What of Hamilton's flash of insight on the bridge? On October 16, 1843, Hamilton was walking across the Royal Canal in Dublin on Brogham Bridge. There, the idea for quaternions hit him. He denied the commutative property of multiplication ($A \times B = B \times A$) and thus was free to develop his new ideas fully. The equation that burst into his head was $i^2 = j^2 = k^2 = ijk = -1$. Fearful he would forget the equation before getting back home, he carved it into the stone bridge with his pen knife, went home to fetch pencil and paper, and returned to copy the equation. This marked the only time in mathematics history that a new equation was carved in stone at its very inception.

It is easier to gain forgiveness than to get permission.

Grace Murray Hopper

For much of her life, Grace Murray Hopper (1906–1992) was developing innovative ideas that were not supported by the establishment. According to Hopper, there were many occasions when she went ahead with her ideas and sought "forgiveness" later, rather than getting "permission" ahead of time.

Grace Murray Hopper was born in New York City and after graduating from Vassar, received a Ph.D. in mathematics from Yale. After a decade of teaching at Vassar, she joined the Naval Reserve in 1943 to work with intelligence operations. During her early years with the Navy, Hopper became involved with computers and computer programming.

In the late 1950s, Hopper observed, "There are a lot of people who don't like symbols, they use words—and so I said, 'Let's write the program in English, and I'll write a program that translates the English words into machine code.'" The result was the first user-friendly computer language using common English. Hopper named it COBOL for Common Business Oriented Language.

Hopper continued to work with the United States Navy until she was seventy-nine years old. By the time of her retirement, she had been promoted to rear admiral and was the oldest commissioned officer on active duty in the United States Armed Forces. Fittingly, her retirement was held on the *Constitution,* the oldest commissioned warship of the United States Navy. She then joined Digital Computer Corporation, working as a consultant until her death on January 1, 1992.

How fast information can be processed by a computer was crucial to Hopper, since it signaled a new era in mathematics. A sought-after speaker, she often punctuated her talks by brandishing an 11.5-inch piece of wire. This was her way of demonstrating how far electrical information travels in one-billionth of a second in a computer.

It is not knowledge
which is dangerous,
but the poor use of it.

Hrotswitha (hrot SVEE ta)

Hrotswitha

The record of mathematics history is meager at best during Europe's Dark Ages. For the most part, schooling was carried on by the Catholic Church, and the students were mostly men who became priests and monks. Evidence that women received any education, much less education in mathematics, during this time is practically nonexistent. What chance did a woman have for acquiring any education?

The name of one woman surfaces in connection with academics during this time, however: the Benedictine nun Hrotswitha of Gandersheim, who lived in Germany during the tenth century. She is known for her writings on a variety of subjects. Hrotswitha wrote local histories and recorded legends and folk tales for her fellow nuns to read. Her attempts to educate women during this time are unparalleled.

She also wrote about mathematics and science. In science, she seems to have anticipated Newton and Copernicus by writing that the sun is the center of the firmament and its gravitational pull "holds in place the stars around it much as the earth attracts the creatures which inhabit it." In mathematics, she recorded lessons that were typical of the mathematics of the day—a bit of arithmetic and a smattering of geometry. In her writings, she gave four examples of perfect numbers: 6, 28, 496, and 8128. Perfect numbers, first discovered by Pythagoras, are numbers that are the sum of their composite factors plus one (for example, $6 = 2 + 3 + 1$). Hrotswitha was one of the few European mathematicians of her era, and the first female mathematician of modern times.

Reserve your right
to think, for even
to think wrongly
is better than
not to think at all.

Theon to Hypatia (hy PAY sha)

Hypatia

Hypatia (370-415) was "the perfect child." At least that is what her father, Theon, raised her to be—and he probably came as close as any parent could. Hypatia was brilliant, artistic, athletic, and well-traveled.

When Hypatia showed remarkable intelligence as a young child, Theon decided to help her become as perfect as possible. Since Hypatia's mother died when she was a baby, she spent most of her time with her father. Theon, a mathematics professor and later administrator at the University of Alexandria, taught Hypatia everything he knew about mathematics. He also immersed her in formal training of the arts, literature, science, and philosophy. He set out a demanding physical regimen which included rowing, swimming, and calisthenics. Hypatia excelled at everything she did. When she was old enough she traveled to broaden her horizons, attending a school in Athens taught by the great Greek biographer, Plutarch.

Hypatia soon became a well-known scientist and mathematician. In fact, she is known as the first woman mathematician in history. Besides writing many mathematical treatises herself, Hypatia was famous for being able to explain complex mathematical ideas clearly. She became a teacher at the University of Alexandria and surpassed her father in both teaching skill and mathematical ability. Hypatia also invented devices to measure the positions of stars and study astronomy.

With the help of God, and with His precious assistance, I say that algebra is a scientific art.

Omar Khayyám (ky YHAM)

Khayyám

Omar Khayyám (c. 1050–1130) is probably better known as a poet and author of the Rubaiyat (meaning a collection of quatrains, or four-line rhymes), a collection of beautiful poems. He was born in Persia, in what is now Nishapur, Iran, and his name suggests either he or his father was a tentmaker by trade (al-khayyám means "tentmaker").

A story that may or may not be true concerns a young Omar Khayyám and his two friends, Nizam-al-Mulk and Hassan Ben Sabbath. The three boys made a pact that whichever of them first obtained a high rank would then help the other two. Al-Mulk became vizier (a high government official) to Sultan Alp Arslan, and accordingly, his friends asked to share in the vizier's good fortune. Hassan Ben Sabbath asked for a position of power in the government, but Khayyám asked only that he be provided with a yearly stipend so he could devote himself to his poetry and mathematics. Both requests were granted.

Khayyám wrote on a number of mathematical topics. In *Discussion of the Difficulties with Euclid* he considered possible proofs of Euclid's postulate of parallels (this postulate says essentially that only one line can be drawn parallel to a given line through a given point not on this line). He also suggested that π and $\sqrt{2}$ were new types of numbers, in contrast to integers and fractions. Khayyám was the first mathematician to deal with every type of cubic equation that yields a positive root. He solved these cubic equations by using the intersections of conic sections.

Khayyám also revised the existing calendar, suggesting a thirty-three year cycle with eight leap years of 366 days each. Khayyám's calendar is actually more accurate than the Gregorian calendar used today.

What happened to Khayyám's boyhood friend, Hassan Ben Sabbath? After receiving a government post, he then tried to take over the vizier's position. Hassan was ousted and eventually became the head of a band of fanatics who used the castle fortress of Alamut near the Caspian Sea to raid passing caravans. One of the victims of Hassan's band was his boyhood friend, the vizier, Nizam-al-Mulk.

Happy is the man who devotes himself to a study of the heavens … their study will furnish him with the pursuit of enjoyments.

Johannes Kepler

Sometimes clinging stubbornly to an old idea can delay a momentous discovery. Only after discarding such an old idea was Johannes Kepler (1571–1630) able to discover the secrets of the Solar System.

Kepler found the geometry of the Solar System after any number of unsuccessful theories by Pythagoras, Aristotle, and many others over hundreds of years. From the time of the Pythagoreans it was assumed that the planets moved in circles inscribed within regular solids. Kepler began with that view but then discovered that thousands of observations by Danish astronomer Tycho Brahe (1546–1601) did not agree with the conclusions of the Pythagoreans, Aristotle, or anyone else. For several years, Kepler tried to fit Brahe's data to planetary circles but could not. Only after he abandoned the idea of circles did Kepler discover that the true path of the planets around the sun was an ellipse.

Kepler had previously used crude calculus to show the parabola was a limiting curve for an ellipse with one of the focal points moving to infinity. Such thinking enabled him to establish the ellipse with the sun as one focal point in the path of the planets. Kepler also related the speed of a planet's revolution to its distance from the sun and found that the radius from the sun to a planet will sweep out equal areas for equal amounts of time. As the diagram below shows, the speed of a planet around the ellipse will vary so that during any given period of time, the checkered areas must be equal.

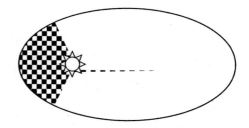

It was left for Newton to fully explain why Kepler's geometry worked, but work it did.

Say what you know, do what you must, come what may.

Sonya Kovalevsky (co va LEV ski)

Kovalevsky

Is it possible to learn calculus at the age of seven? Usually not, but that's how old Sonya Kovalevsky (1850–1891) was when she started getting familiar with calculus. Kovalevsky was born to an aristocratic Russian family. Her father was a general in the Russian army, and when Kovalevsky was very young her family moved to a large house in a remote part of Russia, near the present-day border of Lithuania. Because the house was so large, the funds for repairing and refurbishing ran out before Kovalevsky's bedroom could be wallpapered. The walls were temporarily covered with calculus notes her father had written years before while an undergraduate. Her walls remained covered in calculus notes for a number of years, and every night Sonya Kovalevsky would fall asleep looking at them.

It was not until Kovalevsky was a teenager and enrolled in a calculus class that the notes made any sense. According to her, it seemed as if she had been in a calculus class before; everything seemed so easy and remotely familiar. It is no wonder, since she had spent hundreds of nights reading her father's calculus notes as she fell asleep.

Kovalevsky provided important contributions to mathematics, especially with her research papers on partial differential equations, Abelian integrals, and Saturn's rings. In 1888 she won the prestigious Prix Bordin for her memoir "On the Rotation of a Solid Body About a Fixed Point." She included the quotation, "Say what you know, do what you must, come what may," in this paper.

Kovalevsky was a successful mathematician in a time of great prejudice against women who sought higher education. There were those who refused to accept any woman, even Kovalevsky, as the intellectual equal of a man, much less his superior. When Kovalevsky died, her brain was preserved in alcohol. Four years later it was compared with the brain of the great scientist Hermann von Helmholtz. Kovalevsky's brain was larger, a great disappointment to those who had hoped to prove male superiority by this method!

The most important
questions of life are …
really only problems
of probability.

Pierre Simon de Laplace (la PLAS)

Suppose you had the chance to meet with the Emperor of France, Napoleon Bonaparte, to discuss a new book you had written. How would you respond to a critical comment he made? Marquis Pierre Simon de Laplace (1749–1827) faced that prospect.

Laplace came from a humble background: both of his parents were from peasant families. Little more is known about his childhood since he did all he could to leave the past behind and conceal his lowly upbringing. Any schooling he received was paid for by wealthy families in his hometown who noticed his intellect and ability.

Eventually, Laplace traveled to Paris to make his mark on the world. He wrote a letter of introduction to French mathematician Jean Le Rond d'Alembert (1717–1783) in which he explained some of the mechanics of heavenly bodies. The letter so impressed d'Alembert that he took in Laplace and became his patron. Laplace continued to work at his mechanics of the heavens and from 1799 to 1825 published a five-volume work, *Méchanique Céleste,* which established him as the Newton of France. This great work explained the mathematical physics of the Solar System and established the Solar System's stability beyond anyone's doubt. It was a true triumph for mathematical physics, a mathematics based on applied physics rather than on the elegant proofs of pure mathematics. Laplace also published several books that marked the beginning of modern probability theory.

Laplace lived in during a time of great political instability in France. During his lifetime the government changed from monarchy to republic, to chaos, to an empire, then back to monarchy. Laplace worked with whatever government was in power. He had no strong political convictions but did have strong convictions about mathematics. It was these convictions that might have caused him great grief at the hands of an angry emperor.

Laplace presented a copy of his latest edition of *Méchanique Céleste* to Napoleon, whom he had known for some time and in fact had examined for entrance into the École Militaire when Napoleon was only sixteen. Napoleon's comment about the book was, "You have written this large book on the system of the universe, and have never even mentioned its Creator." Laplace responded, "Sire, I have no need for that hypothesis!" Napoleon told this reply to Joseph Louis Lagrange (a well-known French mathematician and astronomer), who said, "Ah, but it is a beautiful hypothesis; that explains many things."

The theory of probability is at bottom only common sense.

Pierre Simon de Laplace

How could ordering an omelet cost a man his life? The French Revolution was a dangerous time for anyone. Those in hiding had to be especially cautious. French mathematician and aristocrat Marie Jean Antoine Nicholas de Caritat, better known as the Marquis de Condorcet (1743–1794), would learn that lesson too late.

Condorcet was a mathematician and social philosopher who wrote about probability and integral calculus. He assisted in writing the famous *Encyclopédie* of Denis Diderot (1713–1784) and Jean Le Rond d'Alembert (1717–1783). He also advocated public education and the new methods of taxation.

When the Revolution struck, Condorcet embraced its aims and played an active role, serving as president of the Legislative Assembly in 1792. As the Revolution progressed, many members of royalty and the educated class lost their heads to the executioner. Most mathematicians, such as Pierre Simon de Laplace (1749–1827), Gaspard Monge (1746–1818), Joseph Fourier (1768–1830), and Joseph Louis Lagrange (1736–1813) were spared because they could use mathematics to improve the aim of field artillery. Condorcet was likely spared because of his fervent support of the Revolution's aims.

However, increasingly radical forces began to take control, and political moderates became suspect. Condorcet voted against the execution of Louis XVI and was soon considered an outlaw. He fled into hiding, but his appetite for eggs undid him. While traveling incognito, Condorcet entered an inn and asked for an omelet. Unaccustomed to ordering an omelet in such a humble establishment, he did not know what to say when asked how many eggs he would like. He replied, "A dozen." At this, the innkeeper became suspicious and asked about Condorcet's trade. When Condorcet replied he was a carpenter, the innkeeper demanded to see his hands and his identity as an aristocrat was revealed.

Condorcet was taken to prison that night; he did not live to see the dawn. It is unclear whether he was allowed to commit suicide or was poisoned, but in either case, a love of eggs cost a great mathematician his life.

It is unworthy of excellent
men to lose hours like slaves
in the labor of calculation
which could safely be
relegated to anyone else
if machines were used.

Gottfried Wilhelm Leibniz
(LIPE nitz)

If you had invented a calculating machine, the first of its kind, how would you ensure its financial success? Such a task fell to Gottfried Wilhelm Leibniz (1646–1716), considered by many to be the greatest genius of his time— a time which included Sir Isaac Newton!

Leibniz is not a name generally known to mathematics students in the United States, but he is well known in Europe. Leibniz is acclaimed as a coinventor of calculus with Newton. Although not the equal of Newton in mathematics, he was a top-level intellect in many other fields, including metaphysics, history, law, and philosophy.

Leibniz invented a calculating machine that was an improvement on one invented earlier by Blaise Pascal (1623–1662). Pascal's machine could only add and subtract, while Leibniz's new machine could add, subtract, multiply, and divide. It could also determine square roots. During a visit to England, Leibniz showed his calculating machine to the Royal Society. They were so impressed that they elected Leibniz a member of the society on the strength of his invention.

Pascal never realized his hopes for making a fortune with his calculating machine because of his inefficient marketing methods. All of his machines were built by local contractors. If anything went wrong with a calculator—if it needed repair or replacement parts—it had to be sent to Pascal to be fixed. Because this proved expensive and bothersome, Pascal's machines did not sell very well.

Leibniz had a different idea. He marketed his calculating machine in a way similar to a franchise operation of today. Various individuals were given the plans and license to make and sell the machine, with a percentage of their proceeds going to Leibniz. It was a great success. Not only was Leibniz's machine superior to Pascal's machine, so was his method of marketing.

There is no branch
of mathematics
which may not
be applied to the
real world.

Nicolai Lobachevsky
(lo ba CHEFF ski)

What does this quotation lead you to expect about the writings of Nicolai Lobachevsky (1793–1856)? You might predict that all his mathematics would be founded in real-world applications. Nothing could be further from the truth.

Lobachevsky began his academic career as a professor of mathematics in Kazan, Russia, near Siberia. In the early nineteenth century, Siberia was even more remote than it is today. In his early writings, Lobachevsky examined the famous fifth postulate of Euclid's *Elements*. This postulate stated that if a line and a point not on the line are given, then there is only one parallel line that could be drawn through that point. Euclid's original statement seemed too long and complex to be a postulate, so for centuries mathematicians labored to prove it. All attempts had been unsuccessful. Lobachevsky tried his hand at proving it, but he was also unsuccessful.

One way to prove a statement is to deny it. That is, assume the opposing statement is true, then reason from that opposing statement until an obvious contradiction arises. This means the opposing statement cannot be fact. If the opposing statement is not a fact, then the original statement must be true. This is what Lobachevsky tried to do. He used as an opposing statement, "through a point not on the line there are **many** parallels." As Lobachevsky began to draw conclusions from his opposing statement, he derived unusual "facts" such as, "the sum of the angles of a triangle is less than 180 degrees." All of these "facts" fell into place if one ignored the geometry of the real world and considered an entirely new system. Lobachevsky called his new geometry "imaginary geometry."

Was Lobachevsky wrong? Could this be a branch of mathematics that could not be applied to the real world? His work opened the door to other non-Euclidean geometries. At first they seemed as imaginary and useless to the real world as Lobachevsky's "imaginary geometry." It took Einstein and his theory of relativity to find a real-world application for non-Euclidean geometry. It seems Lobachevsky was right. All branches of mathematics can be applied to the real world, even "imaginary geometry."

If I have seen further than [others], it is by standing upon the shoulders of Giants.

Isaac Newton

S ir Isaac Newton (1642–1727) is considered a mathematical and scientific genius. He should have been able to build an entrance in a barn, right? Wrong. As smart as he was, Newton failed at farming.

Ironically, Newton grew up on a farm in Woolsthorpe, England. He was raised by his mother and grandmother (his father had died a few months before Newton's birth). Although receiving some education at a local school, Newton did not display any talent for mathematics. When he was a teenager his mother called him home to manage the farm, but Newton showed very little talent for farming.

One story tells of Newton leading a horse by its bridle out to pasture. Newton became so engrossed in thought that although the bridle slipped off the horse, Newton kept walking to the pasture, bridle in hand, while the horse ran free.

Newton was sent to Cambridge to study. He received his B.A. in 1665, having taken a smattering of mathematics courses without distinguishing himself in any of them. Immediately after his graduation the Great Plague struck England and the Cambridge colleges were closed for the next two years.

Newton returned to his family's farm to wait out the plague. These next two years set Newton on what some call the most intense outpouring of intellectual effort by any one person in history.

During this time Newton began his study of optics, calculus, the binomial theorem, and gravitation. Mathematics and science would never be the same.

After a bad experience with critics when he published his findings on the nature of light, Newton tended to keep his discoveries to himself. It was not until a visit by Sir Edmund Halley (of Halley's comet fame) in 1684 that Newton revealed and finally consented to publish all of his scientific discoveries. The result was the 1687 printing of *Principia,* considered by some people to be the most impressive scientific work ever written. Of Halley's efforts to get Newton to publish *Principia*, Augustus De Morgan wrote, "But for him [Halley], in all human probability, the work would never have been thought of, nor when thought of written, nor when written printed." As De Morgan's statement indicates, Halley even paid for the first printing of *Principia.*

Newton became one of the greatest thinkers of all time. How did he fail to build an entrance in a barn? According to the story, Newton attempted to build special entrances to the barn for some of the farm animals (horses, cows, sheep, cats, and hens). Rather than build one large entrance, Newton built a separate entrance for each animal, essentially filling one entire side of the barn with holes.

I seem to have been only like a boy playing on the seashore, and diverting myself in now and then finding a smoother pebble or a prettier shell than ordinary, whilst the great ocean of truth lay all undiscovered before me.

Isaac Newton

What are the prospects of a boy who was considered an indifferent student? In addition, when he was called back from school to work the farm, he made a mess of it. Finally he was sent back to school, only to return home after two years because of the Great Plague. Would you expect the next two years spent at home would result in the greatest individual output of intellectual achievement in history?

Isaac Newton (1642–1727) was not much of a student when young. Sickly and small at birth, born to a widowed mother, he was sent to live with his grandmother when his mother remarried. His early childhood was marked less by achievement at school than by his inventions of water clocks, mills powered by mice, sundials, and kites. When he finally focused on his schoolwork, it was only in response to a bully's taunting and not from any desire to learn and achieve.

He left school as a teenager to work on his mother's farm after his stepfather died. Constantly daydreaming and wandering from his chores, he was not a good farmer. His uncle suggested sending Newton to Cambridge University. At Cambridge he was undistinguished. It is said that when the university was closed during the plague years, there was only one professor, Isaac Barrow, who even knew Newton by name.

Back at home, Newton continued his habit of daydreaming and thinking about anything but farm matters. There was now a difference. His classes at Cambridge had exposed Newton to mathematics. The books at the local school library and Newton's intellect did the rest. In the space of two short years, Newton laid the groundwork for his invention of calculus, the principles of optics, and the laws of universal gravitation. Any one of these three achievements would class Newton as a thinker of the first rank. To have done all three in such a short time was a feat so unexpected and so unparalleled that is it considered to be the highest achievement of human thought. A man of meager prospects thus became the greatest genius of his time.

There are two
dangerous extremes.

One is to shut reason
out, the other is
to let nothing in.

Blaise Pascal (pass CAL)

French mathematician Blaise Pascal (1623–1662) is best known for coinventing probability theory with Fermat and for his strong religious convictions, for which he gave up his study of mathematics and physics (which he called "games and diversions"). But in 1654 Antoine Gombard, Chevalier de Méré, wrote to Pascal for help with his gambling. De Méré was a man who lived life to the fullest. He was a soldier, an accomplished linguist, and a well-rounded traveler—perfect to have at any gathering of intellectuals. It was at one such gathering that he had met Pascal. De Méré had several questions about chances at dice and had accumulated data from his vast experience of making a living at dice. One of de Méré's questions was, "How many throws of the dice are required to have a better than even chance of throwing a double six?"

The question intrigued Pascal, and he briefly ventured out of his religious studies to communicate with Pierre de Fermat (1601–1665) about probability. The result was Pascal's book *Treatise of Triangle Arithmetic,* which contained Pascal's triangle. Although Pascal's triangle was centuries old by Pascal's time (it is depicted in *Precious Mirror of the Four Elements,* written by Chinese mathematician Chu Sih-Cheih in 1303), the application of binomial expansions to probability earned Pascal the title of cofounder of probability theory with Fermat.

Did all this help de Méré? Most likely. He fancied himself a bit of a mathematician and could have understood Pascal's book, whereas it is unlikely that most of his gambling cohorts could have done so. And Pascal? Except for eight days in 1658, he never again concerned himself with mathematics.

Let no one ignorant
of geometry enter
here.

Plato (PLAY toe)

This curious statement was placed over the door of the first academy in existence, an academy devoted to philosophy and the meaning of life. Why was geometry so important to prospective students? The answer lies with the headmaster of that school, the Greek philosopher Plato (c. 429–c. 348 B.C.).

Plato is known to the world as the foremost Greek philosopher, student of Socrates, and teacher of Aristotle. He founded a school in Athens in a grove of trees named after the owner, Academos. From this name, Plato derived the name of his school, the Academy. The Academy was a center of learning for nearly a thousand years, claiming both commoners and kings as its students.

Plato was known for his philosophy of life, reasoning, ethics, and many other topics. He wrote very little about mathematics. His only original contribution to mathematics (and it may be that he obtained this from an earlier source) is a formula for creating Pythagorean triples, that is, integer values for the sides of a right triangle given any integer value for n, $(2n)$, $(n^2 - 1)$, and $(n^2 + 1)$ are integer sides of a right triangle. The Platonic solids are named for Plato, but they originated with Pythagoras and were only named for Plato because his cosmology utilized them.

Having accomplished so little in the way of original mathematics, why did Plato insist on a knowledge of geometry in all prospective students of the Academy? Plato believed that the thinking and rigor required by mathematics, particularly geometry, was indispensable to the study of philosophy. Plato was a "pure" mathematician. He disliked applied mathematics, believing it did not train the mind as did pure mathematics. According to Plato, anyone who mastered the thinking for geometry was ready to master the thinking required for the philosophy of Plato.

The pursuit of an idea is as exciting as the pursuit of a whale.

Henri Poincaré (poin ca RAY)

Envision sitting in a mathematics classroom without notebook, paper, or pencil. In addition, you are too far back to see the blackboard clearly. This was the usual practice of French mathematician Henri Poincaré (1854–1912).

Poincaré is considered by many to be the last universalist in mathematics. Since his mastery of every topic in mathematics, the discipline has branched and splintered into so many different offshoots that it is impossible for one man to be conversant in all of them. Poincaré published thirty books and over five hundred articles on topics as diverse as probability, differential equations, topology, non-Euclidean geometry, optics, electricity, quantum mechanics, thermodynamics, and the theory of relativity. What is unusual about Poincaré is that he wrote at a level which the common man could understand. His paperback books were widely read, and as a result he was elected a member of the literary section of the French Institute.

As a youth, Poincaré had poor eyesight and even poorer motor skills. He couldn't see the blackboard, and his notes were essentially illegible. It was said he was ambidextrous, since his writing was equally poor with either hand! How did he get along? He had a phenomenal memory! Poincaré would simply listen carefully to the lecture and could then, at his leisure, recreate what was said. Poincaré said he never forgot anything he ever read—he even remembered the page numbers! He used his amazing memory in his own work. He did his best work when he paced back and forth, working out problems in his head. Once he was finished, he put his ideas on paper.

There is an interesting story about Poincaré's poor motor skills. As an adult he took a Binet test, which is designed to establish children's IQ ratings. Poincaré, the greatest living mathematician of his day, was rated at the level of an imbecile because of his inability to perform the simple small motor skills required of a child!

Nature and
Nature's laws
lay hid in night;
God said, Let
Newton be!
and all was light.

Alexander Pope

What college would not be proud to have Sir Isaac Newton (the subject of Pope's quote) on its faculty? Imagine how crowded his lectures would be, with students jammed into the auditorium to hear the great man speak. Suppose he was a member of Congress? How hushed the chambers would become when Newton rose to speak.

Actually, Newton was not a very popular lecturer. As a professor at Cambridge University, Newton was required to lecture once a week. He could choose his topic from "some part of Geometry, Astronomy, Geography, Optics, Statics, or some other mathematical discipline."

In all his years at Cambridge, a grand total of only three students ever attended his lectures. Not that Newton did not try. On numerous occasions, at the appointed time for his weekly lecture, Newton would enter the lecture hall and deliver a lecture whether anyone was there or not!

Newton was also a member of British Parliament for four years. In all that time he gave only one speech. On that one occasion all eyes were on Newton as he rose. What would the great genius say? What topic of the day would he address? He asked to have a window opened.

The essence of all things is numbers.

Pythagoras
(pie THAG oh rus)

Pythagoras

Pythagoras (c. 570–c. 500 B.C.) is one of the most interesting figures in the history of mathematics. He established a school in Croton, in southern Italy. New students had to remain silent during the first three years, and could join in discussions only after the three-year period of silence. Women were not allowed full membership but did attend and participate in the lectures of the Society.

To the Pythagoreans, numbers were viewed as sacred and dominated all of creation. The number one was divine, the root of all other numbers and existence. Even numbers were feminine numbers, and odd numbers were masculine. Four represented justice, since it is the smallest number which fits the configuration of a square. Five represented marriage, because it is a combination of the first feminine and masculine numbers (two and three). Six is a "perfect number," made up of all its divisors and one ($1 + 2 + 3 = 6$).

In the cosmology of Pythagoras, the universe was based on the five regular solids. The cube represented the earth, the pyramid represented fire, the octahedron represented air, the icosahedron represented water, and the dodecahedron represented the universe itself. In addition, the seven known planets were viewed as being contained in gigantic spheres that revolved around the sun. The Pythagoreans felt the planets followed a strict pattern in the "music of the spheres."

Know Thyself.

Thales (TAY lees)

Mathematicians have sometimes been stereotyped as people with their heads in the clouds, lost in thought. While no doubt there have been mathematicians who seem removed from the mundane affairs of life, Thales of Miletus (c. 624–c. 547 B.C.) was not one of them.

Thales is one of the "Seven Wise Men" of antiquity, the only mathematician included among a group of philosophers. He is considered the "Father of Geometry" for his early discoveries and proofs of geometric relationships. For example, he proved that vertical angles are equal in measure and that a diameter divides a circle into two halves.

According to one story, one day Thales was heading to market to sell a load of salt when his donkey lost its footing crossing a stream and fell into the water. When the donkey stood up, its load was considerably lightened since much of the salt had dissolved. When Thales and the donkey came to a second stream, the donkey repeated its routine of falling into the water. This continued until Thales reached the market with a wet donkey and no salt.

Realizing that the donkey had fooled him, Thales came up with a strategy to break the donkey of its stumbling habit. For the return trip, Thales purchased a load of sponges. Upon reaching the first stream on the way back, the donkey again stumbled and fell into the water. This time the load increased, and continued to do so every time the donkey fell into the water. By the time Thales and the donkey returned home, the donkey had learned its lesson.

A man who is not
somewhat of a
poet can never be
a mathematician.

Karl Weierstrass (VEER strass)

Weierstrass

Imagine you are a great mathematics professor. One day, a brilliant twenty-year-old student comes into your office. She has been refused admission to your university because she is a woman, and has come to you for help. Professor Karl Weierstrass (1815–1897) found himself in this situation.

Weierstrass, considered by some to be the greatest mathematics teacher of all time, was born in Germany to a family of modest means. When he performed brilliantly in public schooling, his father sent him to the University of Bonn to study law and finance. The plan was for Weierstrass to become a civil servant and thus be able to provide for his family. Things did not work out as Weierstrass's father planned. Weierstrass spent his four years in Bonn fencing and drinking. He returned home with no degree and no prospects for the future.

Weierstrass enrolled at the Academy of Munster in order to obtain a teaching certificate. He was fortunate to have German mathematician Christoph Gudermann (1798–1852) as an instructor. There were thirteen students in Gudermann's first class but only one student—Weierstrass—in the second class. For the rest of the semester and the subsequent term, Gudermann tutored him in mathematics. Weierstrass received his certificate and taught secondary school from 1841 to 1854. He became a professor relatively late in life and likewise published his mathematical findings at an age when most mathematicians have ceased their creative periods.

Weierstrass was an outstanding teacher, at both the secondary and the college levels. Some of his college students were Georg Cantor (1845–1918), Gustav Mittag-Leffler (1846–1927), Max Planck (1858–1947), and David Hilbert (1862–1943). During his years as a secondary school teacher Weierstrass quietly worked on complex analysis. One story tells about the morning the headmaster found a class full of students and no Weierstrass. Fearing the worst, he hastened to Weierstrass's quarters and found him engrossed in a mathematical problem—he had worked all through the night and was unaware of the time.

Weierstrass eventually became a professor at the University of Berlin, where he helped many budding mathematicians. One of these was the young woman who came into his office asking for help. Her name was Sonya Kovalevsky (1850–1891). Although she was brilliant, she was not allowed to enter the university. Weierstrass appealed to the University Council to admit her, but they refused. He then agreed to privately help Kovalevsky with mathematics. Every Sunday afternoon, and one other time during each week, he gave her his lecture notes and tutored her. This arrangement continued for four years. The master of mathematics teachers had become teacher and patron to one of the greatest woman mathematicians. Unfortunately, Kovalevsky died young of influenza, otherwise she might have achieved even greater honors than her benefactor did.

2

Event of the Week

Can a successful mathematician and academic also be successful in business? Thales of Miletus (c. 624–c. 547 B.C.) proved it was possible over 2,500 years ago. Thales was one of the "Seven Wise Men" of ancient times, included in this select group of philosophers because of his mathematical achievements. As a young man Thales was a very successful merchant who traveled the Mediterranean area extensively. His business successes enabled him to retire early and devote himself to mathematics for most of his adult life.

Thales is credited with discovering and proving the following:

1. Vertical angles are equal in measure.

2. The base angles of an isosceles triangle are equal in measure.

3. A diameter divides a circle into two halves.

Until Thales's time there were no genuine mathematical proofs. Instead, mathematicians presented a number of examples which inductively demonstrated the truth of a statement. For his efforts, Thales is known as the "Father of Geometry."

On May 28, 585 B.C., there was a solar eclipse that some believe was predicted by Thales. While he could not have possibly understood the factors causing an eclipse since he thought the earth was a disk floating on water, Thales did have access to Babylonian records of earlier eclipses. Using their data, some claim he could have established a pattern for eclipses and made his prediction. If he did, it is the first accurate prediction of an eclipse in history.

There was a practical side to Thales' mathematics. While at Alexandria in Egypt, he visited the famous pyramids. By using similar triangles and the shadows of the pyramids, Thales determined their height, the first person to do so by this indirect method. He also used his knowledge of similar triangles to find the distance from the shore to ships at sea.

How did Thales manage to accumulate enough wealth to retire at such a young age? By using logical thinking. One account of Thales' practical reasoning comes from his early manhood. Thales had determined early one spring that there would be an abundant crop of olives. He promptly sold his olive grove and bought up all the olive presses in Miletus. When the abundant harvest came in, Thales had a monopoly on the olive presses and became a rich man.

Pythagoras (570–500 B.C.) is known for probably the most famous theorem in mathematics. In the right triangle below, the sum of the squares of the lengths of the two sides is equal to the square of the length of the hypotenuse, or, as every geometry student knows, $a^2 + b^2 = c^2$.

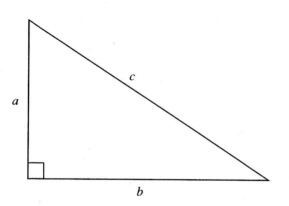

The Pythagorean theorem has been proven by over a thousand different methods, including a proof made by James Garfield only five years before he became the President of the United States.

Was Pythagoras really the discoverer of the theorem that bears his name? The theorem of Pythagoras was known to the Babylonians and Egyptians, at least in special cases such as the 3-4-5 triangle. There is clear evidence the theorem was also known to the Chinese before the time of Pythagoras, so he was not necessarily the first to discover it. It is hard to say whether Pythagoras even originated the theorem.

When he was a young man, Pythagoras left his island home of Samos and traveled for many years before settling in Crotona on the coast of southern Italy. Some of the time he traveled was spent with Thales of Miletus, the "Father of Geometry." The remaining years find Pythagoras in Alexandria, and possibly in Babylon or even India. Some historians make a case for the fact that the theorem made its way from China, then to India, and finally to Babylon, where Pythagoras learned of it. In fact, the Society of Pythagoreans had a rule that any discovery was to be attributed to Pythagoras, so it is not even clear that Pythagoras is in any direct way responsible for the theorem that bears his name.

What we do know about Pythagoras is that he founded a school that elevated the study of numbers to a mystical, religious level. The Pythagoreans discovered the existence of irrationals, the golden section (although they did not call it that), the full application of the Pythagorean theorem, the five regular solids (cube, pyramid, octahedron, dodecahedron, and icosahedron), and the intervals on the musical scale.

Little is known about the personal life of Pythagoras or his followers. They did not write anything down, they were fiercely loyal to one another, and they were extremely secretive. Their symbol was the pentagram, a five-sided star which encompassed the golden section in so much of its structure. Following is a story demonstrating the loyalty of the Pythagoreans to each other.

A Pythagorean was taken quite ill at an inn while on a journey to a distant city. As the Pythagorean's health continued to decline and he neared death, he showed the pentagram to the inn keeper and instructed him to post one on the wall of the inn. Should someone ask about the sign, the innkeeper was to relate the fate of the Pythagorean. When the Pythagorean died, the innkeeper posted the pentagram as instructed. In time, a guest to the inn asked about the pentagram. After the innkeeper related the account, the stranger, obviously a Pythagorean himself, repaid the innkeeper for all monies spent on the deceased Pythagorean's care and burial.

Relatively few translations have been made of Chinese manuscripts into English, and many ancient Asian mathematicians were reluctant to sign and date their works. In many cases, discoveries made in Europe and the Middle East had been found earlier or independently by Asian mathematicians. One such discovery is the Pythagorean theorem.

Chinese mathematician Chang Tshang first wrote a collection of mathematical commentaries in the fourth century B.C., which appears to be a summary of all Chinese mathematical knowledge to that time. The collection was entitled *Chui Chang Suan Shu* and contained nine chapters on the art of mathematics. Three chapters were devoted to surveying and engineering, three chapters to taxation and bureaucratic matters, and the final three chapters to computational techniques, including topics dealing with right triangles. The problems contained in the last chapter involved the Pythagorean theorem. It seems likely that Chang Tshang's problems and his knowledge of the Pythagorean theorem were derived from an earlier source.

Frank Swetz and T. I. Kao of Penn State University make a case for an even earlier development of the Pythagorean theorem. The *Chou Pei Suan Ching* ("The Arithmetic Classic of the Gnomon and the Circular Paths of Heaven") contains a diagram that supports a proof of the Pythagorean theorem although no proof accompanies the diagram. While the text is undated and authorship is unknown, it may date from as long ago as 1100 B.C., which certainly predates Pythagoras (c. 500 B.C.).

Imagine writing a best-selling mathematics textbook that goes through a thousand editions with scarcely any revisions over a period of two thousand years! Yet all the while, your private life remains a mystery. That is exactly the case of Euclid (c. 300 B.C.).

Very little is known about Euclid, the author of *The Elements*. He lived at Alexandria and taught at a university there called the Museum. We know of him because he wrote one of the greatest books ever written. *The Elements* is a collection of all the geometric thought up until that time. It contains thirteen books: books one through six deal with plane geometry, books seven through nine deal with number theory, and books nine through thirteen deal with solid geometry. Although there is nothing original in *The Elements*, Euclid arranged and catalogued the information in a way that determined how students would study geometry for the next two thousand years. From a series of fundamental concepts, common notions, and postulates, Euclid derived all the geometry known to his time. His work is unsurpassed for the huge task involved and for its timelessness.

As late as the middle of the nineteenth century, English school boys were learning ancient Greek or Latin so they could then study Euclid's writing in its original form. It is estimated that Euclid's *Elements*, with over 2000 editions, is the second most widely circulated book in Western civilization after the Bible. In his famous work Euclid told us a great deal about geometry, but nothing about himself. His personal life remains a mystery.

Imagine having such powers of concentration that you continue to work on a mathematics problem while foreign troops sack your city! Archimedes' (287–212 B.C.) concentration was so great that it cost him his life.

Archimedes, along with Karl Friedrich Gauss (1777–1855) and Isaac Newton (1642–1727), is considered one of the three greatest mathematicians in history. His discoveries run the full range of mathematics of his day. He wrote on plane and solid geometry, measurement, arithmetic, problem-solving, and much more. His writings are all original, not a compilation of earlier writers as is so often the case with Greek mathematicians.

Although much of what he wrote is lost, there is still plenty left to put Archimedes in the forefront of mathematicians. In the *Sand Reckoner,* for example, he dealt with enormously large numbers such as $(10^8)^{108}$, and suggested the concept of infinity. When calculating the value of π, Archimedes used inscribed and circumscribed polygons with an increasing number of sides. He finally employed a 96-gon to determine the value of π to be between $3\frac{10}{71}$ and $3\frac{1}{7}$. To do this, Archimedes used what he called a "method," one that anticipates the use of infinitesimals in integral calculus. There are some who feel that with modern notation, Archimedes would have invented the calculus some two thousand years before Newton did.

Archimedes' practical side is shown not only by his discoveries of the principles of the level, the pulley, and the Archimedean screw (a device for bailing water out of ships), but also by his defense of Syracuse. Archimedes spent most of his life in Syracuse, leaving for only a few years to travel and study at Alexandria. In 212 B.C. the city was besieged by Roman troops under General Marcellus. The defense of the city was eventually left to Archimedes and his wondrous machines. Archimedes invented devices for catapulting great stones with nearly one hundred percent accuracy. He designed a huge crane-like device that supposedly could pluck Roman ships right from the harbor. He even developed a way to focus the sun's rays on the Roman ships until they burst into flame. In time, the residents of Syracuse had only to hang an everyday object, like a length of colored rope, out the window to send the Roman fleet scurrying in fright from yet another of Archimedes' inventions.

Eventually, the Romans breached an unwatched gate and entered the city. General Marcellus had given strict orders not to harm Archimedes. Legend has it that when the soldiers came upon Archimedes he was studying a problem he had drawn in the sand. He was so engrossed in the problem he had drawn that he ignored a soldier's order to rise and yield and cursed the soldier for disturbing him. The enraged soldier ran Archimedes through. A tiled floor depicting this scene of Archimedes's death was discovered in the ruins of Pompeii.

Even in death Archimedes celebrated mathematics. His tombstone was carved with a sphere inscribed in a cylinder, to celebrate what Archimedes felt was his greatest achievement: the discovery that the ratio of the volume of the inscribed sphere to the volume of the cylinder was two to three. In 1965, workmen excavating a site for the foundation of a hotel in Syracuse unearthed a tombstone depicting a sphere inscribed in a cylinder!

Imagine writing a dozen outstanding mathematics books and having all but two destroyed. To make matters worse, those remaining two books are partially destroyed as well and are now incomplete. That was the fate of the work of Apollonius of Perga (c. 262–c. 190 B.C.).

Apollonius was born in Asia Minor but traveled to Alexandria, where he was a student and later a teacher. He eventually returned to Asia Minor and settled in Pergamum. Although Apollonius is not well known to many mathematics students, it was Apollonius who earned the title "Great Geometer," rather than Archimedes (287–212 B.C.), who Apollonius saw as a bit of a rival. Apollonius was known by his contemporaries as Epsilon, the Greek letter that stood for the moon, the subject of many of Apollonius' astronomical studies.

Apollonius wrote about a wide range of topics. Some of his books were *Cutting of Ratio; Cutting of Area; On Determinate Sections; Tangencies; Plane Loci;* and *Quick Delivery.* The latter offered some methods for rapid calculations, and some believe it also contained a method for calculating π to 3.1416. All of these books have been lost, and their existence is known only through references by later Greek or Arab mathematicians, who also comment on some of the contents.

Fortunately, Apollonius' greatest work, *On Conic Sections,* has survived. Actually, what has survived is part of *Conic Sections* in Greek and another part in Arabic. About a third of *Conic Sections* has been lost to the ages. However, even an incomplete *Conic Sections* is sufficient to ensure Apollonius a place in mathematics history. In *Conic Sections,* Apollonius redefines *parabola, hyperbola,* and *ellipse* in terms of curves that can be obtained by cutting a cone at various angles. His work begins the merging of algebra and geometry, a task finally completed by René Descartes some eighteen hundred years later. Some suggest that with a modern notation system, Apollonius would have invented analytical geometry.

It fell to Gottfried Wilhelm Leibniz to assign Apollonius his proper place in mathematics history. Leibniz wrote, "He who understands Archimedes and Apollonius will admire less the achievements of the foremost men of later times." It is tantalizing to imagine the exact contents of Apollonius' lost books.

For some mathematicians, their craft has meant fame and fortune. For a few others, such as Hypatia (370–415), it cost them their lives.

Hypatia is known as the first woman mathematician. She was trained by her father, Theon, a teacher and later an administrator at the University of Alexandria. Hypatia received a well-rounded education and took her father's place on the teaching staff of the university. Hypatia wrote many treatises on mathematics, but few have survived to this day. One particular treatise dealt with the conic sections of Apollonius (262–190 B.C.), helping to popularize his work. She also wrote about Diophantine equations and extended the work of Diophantus (c. 250). On the practical side, a letter from Synesius of Cyrene credits her with inventing the astrolab and other scientific devices.

In addition to being a writer of mathematics texts, Hypatia was also an outstanding teacher, renowned for her intellect and her methods. She was held in such high repute that a letter addressed to simply "The Oracle" (an oracle is a person of great wisdom) would be delivered to her! Eventually, Hypatia's popularity as a mathematics teacher led to her untimely death.

Hypatia's science and scientific methods were a threat to the dominant Christian religion of Alexandria. Her rationalism was in direct conflict with some of the Christian sect's teachings. The situation became more acute when Cyril became archbishop of the Alexandrian Church in 412. He began an active campaign against the scientific methods of Hypatia, eventually stirring up a mob of people who dragged her from her chariot and tortured her to death in 415.

The invention of zero marks one of the milestones in mathematics history. The name of the mathematician who thought of the concept is unknown, but the great Indian mathematician who brought zero to the Western world was Brahmagupta (c. 600–c. 660). Brahmagupta's work, brought to the court of Caliph al-Mansur in Baghdad in 760, introduced the Hindu numerals to the Arabic-speaking world. From there, zero reached Western Europe about five hundred years later.

Brahmagupta was born around the year 600 in India. Not much is known about his personal life or the extent of his work in mathematics, except for his book *Brahma-sphuta-sidd' hanta* ("Revised System of Brahma"). This book is essentially a book on astronomy, but two of its chapters deal with mathematics.

Besides writing about zero, Brahmagupta listed the rules for multiplying signed numbers and presented equations with negative solutions. He also introduced the principle that every positive number has two square roots, one positive and the other negative. Brahmagupta dealt with a bit of geometry in his book, presenting the formula for the area of a cyclic (inscribed in a circle) quadrilateral.

The area of this quadrilateral is found by using the following formula:

$A = \sqrt{(s-a)(s-b)(s-c)(s-d)}$, where s represents half the perimeter. He further found a formula for each of the diagonals, m and n.

$$m^2 = \frac{(ab + cd)(ac + bd)}{ad + bc} \text{ and } n^2 = \frac{(ac + bd)(ad + bc)}{ab + cd}$$

The most noteworthy mathematical aspect of his book is that Brahmagupta not only wrote about zero, but also anticipated that *kha-cheda* ("the quantity with zero as the denominator") will have a value that is infinitely large.

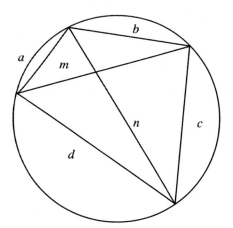

Abu l-Rayhan al-Burini (973–1040) was an Islamic mathematician who wrote on many different subjects. He was born on September 4, 973, in the same area of what is present-day Iran as mathematician al-Khwarizmi (c. 825), and he used al-Khwarizmi as a role model. His early youth was spent hiding or fleeing from any one of the four armies fighting over his hometown.

By the age of thirty al-Biruni had written books on mathematics and science, as well as *The Calendar of Ancient Nations*. This last book contained information that enabled Islamic astronomers to convert calendars of other nations to the Islamic calendar, meaning that the predicted date of an eclipse from an ancient calendar could be converted to an Islamic date.

Al-Biruni became a diplomat, serving as spokesman for the local ruler, Shah Abu l-Abbas Ma'mun. In spite of al-Biruni's "tongue of silver and gold," the shah was killed and al-Biruni was taken prisoner by the Sultan Mahmod. In time, al-Biruni gained the sultan's confidence, and he was allowed to travel the sultan's empire. He reached India by the year 1030.

Upon his return from India, al-Biruni wrote the books that established him as the greatest applied mathematician of the Arab-speaking world. His masterwork, *The Determination of the Coordinates of Localities*, contained a map of the entire known world. The map improved on Ptolemy's map of about a thousand years earlier and was more accurate in its representation of the Mediterranean area. In his map al-Biruni determined that each degree on the meridian was equal to 56 miles, a value closer to the actual value than Ptolemy's.

Al-Biruni published a table of sine and tangent values correct to four decimal places. He also published *At-Tafhaim Le Avaele Snatte Tanjim,* the first mathematics text ever written for the general public. Al-Biruni followed this work in 1040 with *Gems*, a science text that described a variety of stones and listed the specific gravity of each. At the age of eighty, al-Biruni published *Pharmacology*, a text which listed 720 drugs, their origins, and their therapeutic value. *Pharmacology* contained the name of each drug in Greek, Arabic, Persian, Syrian, and local dialects. In all, al-Biruni wrote over 153 works on topics ranging from geometry, algebra, and arithmetic to astronomy and optics.

One example of the applied mathematics of al-Biruni occurred in 997 when he was living in the city of Kath (on the Oxus River in ancient Persia) and fellow mathematician Abu'l-Wafa was living in Baghdad. By utilizing their observations of an eclipse of the moon, al-Biruni was able to determine the longitudinal difference between the two cities and use this information for his great map.

Bhaskara Acharya (1114–1185), was the last Medieval Hindu mathematician. His greatest work, *Lilavati,* is known not only for its content, but also for how it got its title. Bhaskara dedicated it to his daughter, Lilavati, after she missed her only opportunity to marry.

The book *Lilavati* and Bhaskara's other famous work, *Vija-Ganita,* deal with quadratic equations, mensuration, Pythagorean triples, and geometric progressions. In his writings on quadratic equations, Bhaskara discussed is now known as the Pell equation, named after John Pell (1611–1685). A Pell equation has the form $x^2 = 1 + py^2$. Bhaskara found the following integral solutions for p: 8, 11, 32, 61, and 67. To get some sense of the mathematics involved with Bhaskara's solutions, consider the following numbers: if $p = 61$, then $x = 1,776,319,049$ and $y = 22,615,390$.

Bhaskara also commented on division by zero. He wrote, "The fraction of which the denominator is cipher is termed an infinite quantity," thus anticipating the theory of limits.

Bhaskara was also an astrologer. He was so confident in his skills as such that he had determined the exact day and hour for his daughter's wedding. When the wedding day arrived, Bhaskara's daughter was so anxious to be wed on the appointed hour that she kept checking the water clock every few minutes. No one noticed when a pearl fell from her headdress into the water, plugging up the timing hole. The pearl lay unnoticed until long after the set hour had passed, along with her opportunity to be wed. To comfort his distraught daughter, Bhaskara titled his greatest work with her name, Lilavati.

What would you think of a mathematician who signed all his works with the name "Blockhead"? That is exactly what Leonardo of Pisa (c. 1175– c. 1258), better known as Fibonacci, did. Why would he do such a thing?

Fibonacci was born to a merchant in the Italian city of Pisa. He traveled with his father throughout the Mediterranean, including Arab ports in North Africa and on the eastern end of the Mediterranean Sea. It is likely he learned a great deal of mathematics from the Arab clients with whom his father did business.

Fibonacci is best known for his book *Liber Abaci,* which is the first book in Western Europe to advocate the use of the Hindu-Arabic number system we use today. An earlier book by Gerbert of Aurillac (c. 945–1003), *Rules for Computation with Numbers on the Abacus,* used a positional system and numerals from 1 to 9, but not zero. Gerbert probably became acquainted with Hindu-Arabic numbers while serving the Catholic Church in northern Spain. Gerbert, who eventually became Pope Sylvester II, used the abacus in Spain and then introduced it into Western Europe.

In the first chapter of *Liber Abaci,* Fibonacci opened with the words, "There are nine figures of the Indians 1 2 3 4 5 6 7 8 9. With these nine figures and the symbol 0 which in Arabic is called *zephirum,* any number can be written as will be demonstrated below." His book was essentially a book of calculating, but it also dealt with linear and quadratic equations. It is primarily a translation of Arabic mathematics into Latin for use by Europeans. *Liber Abaci* also contains the famous rabbit problem, the solution of which is the Fibonacci sequence: the ratio of two numbers of the sequence approaches the value of the golden ratio or golden section. No copies of the original edition of *Liber Abaci* survive, but a copy of the 1228 edition does exist. Fibonacci also published *Libre Quadratorum* in 1225, a text that reviews the quadratic equations of Diophantus.

Fibonacci was a fair mathematician in his own right. In a contest with John of Palermo, who was the court mathematician of Emperor Frederick II of the Norman kingdom of Sicily, Fibonacci solved the following equation: $x^3 + 2x^2 + 10x = 20$ to get the value $x = 1.3688081075$. It is unclear whether Fibonacci really solved this on his own or found a similar problem in his Arab manuscripts, but the answer, correct to eleven places after the decimal, was remarkable for the times.

Why did Fibonacci use the name "Blockhead" to sign his books and papers? It is believed that the name was first used by those who opposed Fibonacci's new numbering system but that he eventually adopted it himself to show the world what a "blockhead" could do with the new Hindu-Arabic numerals. Surprisingly, the new system did not immediately win out over Roman numerals. In fact, in 1298 the city council of Florence, Italy, forbade the use of the Hindu-Arabic numbering system. Why? For two reasons. First, it was easier to forge some of the numbers (for example, 0 can easily be changed to 6). Second, in contrast to calculations done on an abacus with Roman numerals, calculations with the Hindu-Arabic system were done on hard-to-find, expensive paper, which was then discarded. However, even the Florentines eventually came around.

Can you imagine writing math calculations on a table covered with dust? Once, methods for solving mathematical problems were limited to what you could do on a dust table, a table on which figures were drawn in the dust or sand. Then a new technology changed the way mathematicians calculated problems—paper. Jamshid al-Kashi (c. 1360–1429) was one mathematician to use this new technology to design his method of calculating square roots.

Al-Kashi was the last of the outstanding Islamic mathematicians of the Middle Ages. Islamic scientists of the Middle Ages came from many different countries, but all wrote in Arabic, the leading language of science at that time. Al-Kashi was born in Kashan, Persia (Iran), where he grew up in a poverty-stricken family. By 1414 he had moved to Samarkand (now in Uzbekistan in the former U.S.S.R.) and become the official mathematician in the court of his patron, Ulugh Beg.

Among al-Kashi's accomplishments is the determination of the value of π to sixteen places by using Archimedes' method of inscribed and circumscribed polygons. In his calculations he used polygons with 805,306,368 sides! Al-Kashi wanted a value so accurate that when he calculated the circumference of the universe, his value would not differ "by the width of a horse's hair" from the actual length.

In *The Calculator's Key*, al-Kashi published a systematic discussion of decimal fractions that contained an algorithm for finding the fifth root of a number. He demonstrated his method by finding the fifth root of 44,240,899,506,197. He also discussed a method for solving cubic equations using conic sections. His book became the standard mathematics text in Persia for the next three hundred years.

Al-Kashi's method of calculating square roots was designed to be used with writing paper. Samarkand was one of the first places in Central Asia to import paper from the Chinese, and by al-Kashi's time mathematicians had been using paper and ink for several hundred years. Earlier methods for finding the square root were designed to be used on a dust table. Naturally, figures were written in a large characters, and lack of room required the erasing of earlier steps in order to write out subsequent parts of the problem. In contrast, al-Kashi's new method anticipates the pencil-and-paper algorithms of today.

Picture a man who has faced a lifetime of adversity, a man who has seen one tragedy after another. He finally makes a breakthrough discovery in mathematics only to have it stolen from him by another. This is the story of one of the most tragic figures in the history of mathematics, Nicolo Fontana (c. 1500–1557), better known as Nicolo Tartaglia.

Tartaglia was a boy of twelve when French troops sacked his town of Brescia in northern Italy. Tartaglia's father was killed, and Nicolo was struck on the mouth and jaw by a swordsman, leaving him with a horrible disfigurement. As he grew to maturity, Tartaglia grew a full, lush beard to hide his scars, but he never overcame the stuttering caused by his injury. The name *Tartaglia* means "stammerer" and was given him by his critics. In later life, Tartaglia adopted the name for his own and even signed his works with it. Tartaglia was an able mathematician who developed the applied mathematics for ballistics, thus helping to replace swords and sabers with cannons.

Tartaglia had at least one bright moment in his life—his discovery of the method for solving an equation of the type $x^3 + px = q$. Armed with a formula which solved such equations, Tartaglia was able to win a number of mathematics contests.

His success attracted the attention of one Hieronimo Cardano (1501–1576), born on September 24, 1501, a renowned doctor and mathematician.

Cardano beseeched Tartaglia by letter to reveal his formula so Cardano could include it in his new book. Tartaglia refused, perhaps realizing that credit received in a footnote is not equal to the credit earned by an author of a book that expounds on a discovery. When Tartaglia refused to divulge his secret, Cardano traveled to meet Tartaglia and renewed his plea. Tartaglia's diary contains their subsequent conversation, including Cardano's vow to "not only never to publish your discoveries, but . . . to note them in code so that after my death no one will be able to understand them." On the basis of this assurance, Tartaglia revealed his formula to Cardano.

Tartaglia's worst fears were soon realized when Cardano published his masterpiece *Ars Magna*. Although he credited Tartaglia in three separate places for originating the formula and stated that "only with the help of my good friend Tartaglia" was he able to produce the book, Tartaglia's formula and fame were credited to Cardano.

Tartaglia spent the rest of this life in futile effort trying to restore the formula to its proper owner. He died an embittered old man on December 15, 1557. Cardano, who was also an astrologer, predicted the date of his own death, then ensured the accuracy of his prediction by committing suicide on September 21, 1576.

Imagine a year that is missing ten whole days, a year with only 355 days. It happened in Europe in 1582. The explanation is an interesting account in the history of mathematics.

By 1572 the Julian calendar had been used in Western Europe for over sixteen hundred years. It was named for Julius Caesar, who had commissioned a new calendar to replace an older, inaccurate one. The Julian calendar year was 365.242199 days long compared to the actual length of a year, 365.25 days. The seemingly minor discrepancy amounted to a difference of eleven minutes and forty-four seconds per year.

In 1545 the Council of Trent authorized the pope to revise the Julian calendar, which was about ten days out of line with real time. No action was taken until 1572, however, when Pope Gregory XIII began the process of calendar revision under the direction of the Jesuit mathematician Christopher Clavius (1537–1612). Clavius's recommendation was to restore the calendar to its true position by eliminating ten days. The revision made to the Julian calendar was simply a change in the leap year rule. Leap years are still counted every four years, but with one exception. If a century year is not divisible by four hundred, then it is not a leap year. That means the year 2000 will be a leap year, but the years 2100, 2200, and 2300 will not be leap years.

The switchover from the old Julian calendar to the new Gregorian calendar began in the Catholic countries of Europe in 1582. By 1587 most of them had made the change. In 1582, the day after October 4 was October 15. Because England was not a Catholic country, it did not institute the change to the Gregorian calendar until 1752. Relatively speaking, England was not so slow in making the switchover. Turkey switched to the Gregorian calendar in 1908, China did so in 1912, and Greece switched over in 1923!

Will we have to revise the Gregorian calendar some time in the future? Probably not. The Gregorian calendar is off real time by less than thirty seconds per year, and it will take about 3,323 years to add an extra, unnamed day.

While serving King Henry IV during France's war with Spain, French mathematician François Viète (1540–1603) was accused of "sorcery." Viète broke Spanish codes containing ciphers that were several hundred characters long. He was so proficient at deciphering the enemy's messages that King Philip II of Spain complained to the pope that the French (namely Viète) were using magic "contrary to the practice of the Christian faith." If Viète had served Philip II instead, Henry IV would likely have made a similar charge.

Viète was an important link in the development of our algebraic symbols. It was Viète who, in *In Artem Analyticam Isagoge* (1591), first used letters to represent numbers. In Viète's scheme of symbols, consonants stood for unknown values, and vowels for known values. This seemingly simple concept had dramatic consequences for the development of mathematics. With this new concept, an entire class of equations could be examined with a single expression, such as $xa + be = c$, whereas in the past each equation of a class was considered separately since they each contained different coefficients. Subsequently, rapid advances were made in the development of algebra.

Viète also wrote on trigonometry, geometry, and arithmetic and was the first mathematician to advocate using decimal fractions, although he never developed a notation for decimals. His notation was a bit cumbersome: A^2 was expressed as A *quadrivium* and A^3 as A *cubus* in his equations.

In a contest with national pride at stake, Adrianus Romanus, a mathematician from the Low Countries, gave Viète a forty-five-degree equation to solve. At first, Viète could find only two solutions, but then he saw a connection to trigonometry and produced twenty-one additional answers—finding all of the positive values. He was unable to find the negative solutions, however. The mathematics necessary to derive negative solutions was not developed until the time of René Descartes (1596–1650).

One of the most interesting stories in the history of mathematics is about the mathematician John Napier (1550–1617), a thief, and a "magic" rooster.

Napier lived the quiet life of a nobleman in Scotland as the Laird of Merchiston. He spent most of his life at his ancestral home, rarely leaving his beloved Scotland. In spite of his relative isolation, Napier invented one of the great labor-saving techniques in mathematics, the logarithm.

In 1614 Napier published *A Description of an Admirable Table of Logarithms* to nearly universal acclaim. The use of logarithms enabled tedious multiplication and division to be done as easily as addition and subtraction. This was such a benefit that Pierre Simon Laplace (1749–1827) said that "by shortening the [mathematical] labors, [Napier's logarithms] doubled the life of an astronomer." A sidelight to the invention of logarithms was *Napier's bones*. This was a device made of two lengths of bone or wood (or occasionally, ivory) inscribed with numbers. When the lengths were aligned properly, they could be used for calculations in the manner that a slide rule (developed soon afterward by Henry Briggs (1561–1630)) is used.

And the "magic" rooster? Napier used it when he discovered that one of his workers was stealing from him. Napier lined up all of his servants and told them he had a "magic" rooster that was able to determine the thief. The coal-black rooster was put in a darkened cellar. Each servant had to enter the cellar and pet the rooster. When the thief petted the rooster, it would identify him by crowing. Unbeknownst to the workers, Napier had covered the rooster with soot. The thief was the one servant who was afraid to pet the rooster and thus was the one servant who emerged from the cellar with clean hands!

Johannes Kepler (1571–1630) was born in Stuttgart, Germany, to a family who encouraged him to enter the Lutheran ministry. He had contracted smallpox at the age of four and suffered from crippled hands and poor vision. The ministry seemed an ideal career for a man who could not perform hard physical labor. He attended the University of Tübingen with the ministry in mind. Fate, however, altered his plans. Clerical opposition to a paper he wrote in support of the Copernican Solar System was enough to convince Kepler that the ministry was not for him, so he became a mathematics teacher. From all reports he was not a very inspiring teacher. His first year he had only twelve students, and his second year he had none. In 1599 he left the teaching field and took a position as assistant to the great Danish astronomer, Tycho Brahe (1546–1601), who was the court astronomer for Rudolf II, Holy Roman Emperor. When Brahe died suddenly in 1601, Kepler took his position.

Kepler made his name as an astronomer. When he was growing up, the controversy of the new Copernican theory was swirling throughout Europe. At the same time, the Catholic church was fighting to keep such radical ideas from the people. In Italy, Galileo would be placed under house arrest by the Vatican (the government of the Roman Catholic church) for agreeing with Copernicus that the earth revolved around the sun, and not the other way around, as the church taught.

Although Kepler had the advantage of living in Germany where there was more freedom to write and reason about scientific matters, his experience in Tübingen showed how deep opposition to the Copernican theory ran. Kepler also knew of Copernicus's persecution.

In spite of this, in 1609 he published *Nova Astronomica,* which contained two of his three laws dealing with the paths of planets around the sun. In 1619 he revealed his third law, which together with the first two laws finally settled the question of the paths of the planets and readied the world for Isaac Newton's mathematics, which would explain it all. Besides breaking with the ruling church in the matter of the earth revolving around the sun, Kepler broke new ground when he stated that the planets move in ellipses around the sun, with the sun as one of the focus points. (He coined the word *focus.*)

Fame and fortune were never Kepler's, however. He was never well rewarded for his astronomy or his mathematics and was reduced to casting horoscopes for the nobility in order to survive. His wife went mad and died, his mother was arrested for witchcraft, and his son fell victim to smallpox. Kepler even claimed to be inhabited by the reincarnated soul of Pythagoras.

Although Kepler hesitated at times to make his findings public, he finally did so in the face of persecution and great personal problems.

On August 26, 1572, French mathematician Peter Ramus (1515–1572) was assassinated for what some believe were his personal opinions about mathematics. How could mathematics be reason enough to assassinate someone?

Peter Ramus, also known as Pierre de La Ramus, was a French mathematician best known for his teaching and writings on logic. Ramus first began to teach at the College du Mans in Paris, where he tried to revise the logic of Aristotle, the predominant teaching and reasoning structure of the day. In Ramus's view, logic was a two-sided argument rather than a single logical presentation of a thought process, as Aristotle taught. Besides being a professor, Ramus was a prolific writer, flooding France with pamphlets, papers, and books advocating his revised logic.

Ramus met with increasing resistance from advocates of Aristotelian logic, and in 1544, King Françoise I removed him from the college and supressed his writings. In 1547 the ban was lifted by the new king, Henry II, and by 1551 Ramus was a professor of logic and philosophy at the College de France.

In 1561 Ramus converted to Protestantism. The opposition had expanded by virtue of his unrelenting attacks on Aristotle, and now Ramus was also criticizing the Roman Catholic church. On August 26, 1572, two days after the St. Bartholomew's Day massacre of Protestants by Catholic forces in France, Ramus was himself assassinated.

The man who some consider the greatest mathematician of his time never wrote a mathematics book and by vocation was a lawyer, not a mathematician. How could such a man be a great mathematician? The life of Pierre de Fermat (1601–1665) answers this question.

Fermat was born on August 17, 1601 near Toulouse, France, to a leather merchant and his wife. He had the normal public schooling, then went to the University of Toulouse to pursue the vocation that was a tradition in his wife's family, a public service lawyer. By 1630 he was a member of the Commission of Registrants in Toulouse, and in 1648 he became a king's councilor in the local parliament. By all accounts, Fermat handled his responsibilities admirably.

In spite of all his responsibilities, Fermat found time to engage in his hobby of mathematics. He published only one pamphlet in his lifetime, stating, "Whatever of my works is judged worthy of publication, I do not want my name to appear there." Although Fermat did not publish his findings, he communicated with nearly every great mathematician of his day on a variety of mathematical topics, including analytical geometry, number theory, geometry, differential calculus, probability, and trigonometry. He proposed problems, offered solutions, and presented statements of fact that he had proven, challenging others to do so as well. It appears that Fermat visualized analytical geometry before René Descartes (1596–1650) and had much of the notion of differential calculus in hand years before Isaac Newton (1642–1727) invented it. He is also credited with establishing the field of mathematical probability with Blaise Pascal (1623–1662). Many of Fermat's discoveries remained to be found in his personal notes after he died. Some discoveries were left to others to prove, since Fermat made a practice of writing to fellow mathematicians about theorems he had proven without including the proofs.

How did Fermat manage to spend so much time on mathematics while serving in a demanding position as solicitor for the king? The answer lies in the position a solicitor held in society. As a solicitor, Fermat was expected to be cautious in his private life and to avoid getting involved with local social activities. Thus, Fermat had time to devote himself to his real love, mathematics. Dubbed "Prince of the Amateurs" for his achievements in mathematics, Fermat is considered the last great mathematician to pursue mathematics as simply a recreation and not a vocation.

Evangelista Torricelli (1608–1647) experienced firsthand how the demonstration of a simple scientific principle could put one's life at risk.

Torricelli, born on October 15, 1608, in Faenza, Italy, was Galileo's most famous student, eventually serving as his secretary from 1641 to 1642. Like Galileo, Torricelli was interested in the practical applications of mathematics. He proved Galileo's conjecture about the area under a cycloid, using methods involving indivisibles that anticipated the calculus Isaac Newton would soon invent. In contrast, Galileo cut up and weighed pieces of wood to support his conjecture.

One of Torricelli's mathematical discoveries, Fermat's point, was made in response to a request by French mathematician Pierre de Fermat (1601–1665). Fermat's point is the point located at a minimum total distance from all three vertices of an acute triangle. In the diagram below, $PA + PB + PC$ is at a minimum when point P is Fermat's point.

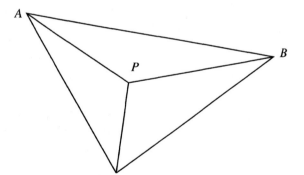

In mathematical terms, the point is known as the isogonic point.

Torricelli's masterwork in mathematics was the *Opera Mathematica* (1644), which dealt with the geometry of figures in motion. Torricelli is best known for his work with the flow and pressures of liquids, the acceleration of objects, the paths of projectiles, and the invention of the barometer. The invention of the barometer nearly cost Torricelli his life. Most liquid barometers use mercury, but Torricelli decided to erect a barometer that used water to show the atmospheric pressure.

At sea level air pressure will support an enclosed column of water roughly thirty feet tall. Torricelli built such a barometer in Florence and placed a mannequin on top of the water so the water level could be seen by passersby. When the mannequin dropped, the falling pressure indicated an approaching storm, while a rising mannequin indicated good weather. Unfortunately for Torricelli, the townsfolk of Florence thought the mannequin (and thus Torricelli) was controlling the weather and gave serious consideration to burning Torricelli and his mannequin at the stake. Fortunately for Torricelli, rational thinking prevailed and his discovery of barometric pressure did not cost him his life.

In 1633 Galileo Galilei (1564–1642) was charged with heresy (a religious belief that is opposes the doctrine of a specific church) for teaching Copernicus's theory that the sun, rather than the earth, was the center of the Solar System. Galileo did not think this theory should contradict the doctrines of the church. As he said, "The Bible teaches how to go to heaven, not how the heavens go." Galileo was not the only scientist/mathematician to place the sun at the center of the Solar System, but he was the first to publish his conclusions in the language of the common people—Italian, in this case—rather than in scholarly Latin.

As early as 1616 the Catholic Church ordered Galileo not to hold to or teach such a theory. However, the election of Pope Urban VIII in 1623 brought about an apparent change of policy for the Catholic Church and Galileo felt free to publish his *Dialogue Concerning the Two Chief World Systems* in 1632. The book made an excellent case for the Copernican Solar System. Galileo had been mistaken about the church's change of attitude, however, and he was accused of heresy.

Galileo was found guilty by the church court. Seventy years old, ill, and threatened with torture, Galileo fell to his knees and recanted the Copernican Solar System with the sworn statement, "I do abjure … the said errors and heresies … I shall never again speak … such things." Legend has it that upon arising from his knees he muttered under his breath, "Nevertheless, the earth does move!" He was sentenced to house arrest until his death nine years later.

In 1822 the church's ban on the works of Galileo was lifted. In 1979 Pope John Paul II appointed a commission, and on March 1, 1984, the Vatican newspaper *L'Observatore Romano* said, "The so-called heresy of Galileo does not seem to have any foundation, neither theologically nor under canon law." Finally, in 1992, Pope John Paul II declared that the church was mistaken in condemning Galileo.

What type of funeral would you give the greatest universal genius of your century, a man who spent his adult life as a diplomat, serving king and country? No doubt you would conceive of something much better than what Gottfried Wilhelm Leibniz (1646–1716) received when he died.

Leibniz was born on July 1, 1646, in Leipzig, Germany. His father was a university professor who died when Leibniz was only six years old. Left to educate himself, Leibniz mastered Latin by age eight and Greek by age twelve. By this point, his intellectual abilities were obvious to the rest of the family, and he was given full access to his father's extensive library. By age twenty he had mastered philosophy, metaphysics, and a good deal of mathematics. He was refused a Ph.D. from Leipzig University on the grounds that he was too young but was awarded one from the University of Altdorf the same year. Soon after, he wrote an essay advocating an historical approach to the study of law and dedicated it to the Elector at Mainz. His essay was so well received that he was given a position in the diplomatic service, where he served various local rulers for the rest of his life.

During his life Leibniz wrote and published articles about so many topics it is difficult to imagine how one person could be capable of achieving such heights in such varied disciplines. Leibniz was a master at Sanskrit, German, French, English, and other languages; he was an expert in jurisprudence; and he wrote on philosophy, metaphysics, and mathematics.

Leibniz invented the calculus independently of Isaac Newton (1642–1727) during the years between 1673 and 1678. Some believe that he had access to some of Newton's notes on the subject (Newton invented the basics of the calculus in 1665, but published nothing on the subject), but most believe Leibniz was a true coinventor of the calculus. Leibniz continually tinkered with the notation of his calculus, finally developing the notation that, while virtually unchanged, is used today.

Leibniz is best described by what one historian wrote. "It seems incredible that one head could have been responsible for all the thoughts, published and unpublished, which Leibniz committed to paper." Leibniz never did receive the fame and fortune that should have been his. His funeral was attended by a grand total of one person, his secretary. In the words of a contemporary, he was "buried like a robber [rather] than what he really was, the ornament of his country." Several years passed before his gravestone was finally inscribed.

The foremost mathematician of France, the greatest mathematician in Europe, was sitting in a darkened, unheated room at five o'clock in the morning in a land he described as "a land of bears, amongst rocks and ice." How did French mathematician René Descartes (1596–1650) end up so far from home and in such frigid conditions?

Descartes was born near Paris and received a quality education at the Jesuit school of La Fléche. He excelled in his studies and received a law degree from the University at Poitiers. After spending some time in the military, prompted more by a desire to travel than by a thirst for military adventure, Descartes settled down to a life of mathematics.

Descartes's desire was to show a rational connection between all fields of science by means of a chain of reasonings that he called "the Method." In Descartes's view all of nature could be explained as the inner workings of complex machinery. He conceived of a plan of universal science, in which all problems could be solved by reason and self-evident intuition, and which could be unified with philosophical truth into a single system of thought. He synthesized all of these thoughts in his masterwork, *Discourse de la Méthode,* which he published in 1637 to great acclaim. His popularity was so great that he frequently moved to escape the adulation of frequent visitors.

In 1649 Descartes received an invitation from Queen Christina to come to Sweden and tutor her in mathematics. He was hesitant, but the queen sent an admiral accompanied by a fully decked-out warship to escort him to Sweden. It was an offer Descartes couldn't refuse. After six months of orientation and settling in, his tutoring regimen began.

The young Queen Christina decided to be tutored when she arose, at five o'clock in the morning. In addition, the library had to be unheated so that Christina could comfortably exercise while she was being tutored. Descartes had been accustomed to a life of lying in bed until he felt like rising, usually not until close to noon. His new schedule was too taxing for him. On the morning of February 1, 1650, Descartes caught a cold that developed into pneumonia. He was dead within a week.

When Descartes's body was returned to France for a final burial, the official who arranged the funeral kept his right hand as a memento of the great man!

Blaise Pascal (1623–1662), born in Clemont-Ferrard, France, has been dubbed the "greatest could-have-been" in the history of mathematics. He could have been an outstanding mathematician, perhaps the best of all time, but for a life-changing experience.

Pascal's home life was relatively pleasant. The children were taught at home by their father, who believed in curiosity as a guiding force in learning. He never forced the children to learn, but waited for the curiosity that all children have to guide his instruction. According to Pascal's father, children should not be taught mathematics until they are fifteen years old. For Pascal, however, fifteen was much too late, and he started in on mathematics by himself. By twelve he had proven to himself the thirty-second proposition of Euclid. Upon seeing this, his father relented and gave him a copy of *The Elements*, which Pascal devoured.

When he was sixteen years old, Pascal wrote a pamphlet, *The Geometry of Conics,* which was so well thought out that René Descartes (1596–1650) refused to believe a sixteen-year-old was capable of such mature thought. In this pamphlet, Pascal proved several theorems involving a mystic hexagon inscribed in conic sections. By age eighteen Pascal had invented the first calculator that could accurately add and subtract by a series of wheels and gears.

In the brief time he delved into mathematics, Pascal made discoveries in geometry, barometric pressure, flows of liquids, and binomial expansion by means of what has become known as Pascal's triangle. He is also known as the cofounder of probability theory with Pierre de Fermat (1601–1665).

When Pascal was twenty-three years old, his father became ill and was assisted back to health by two men who had converted to a new, strict religion called Jansenism. Soon Pascal and his whole family were Jansenists, and increasing pressure was brought on Pascal to drop his mathematics—which he eventually did. One story attributes Pascal's final decision to a horse accident. He was driving a carriage across the bridge over the Seine River at Neuilly when the horses veered off the bridge, pulling the carriage with them. At the last moment the carriage broke free and stayed on the bridge, but the horses fell to their deaths. Could this brush with death have been what turned Pascal to a religious life? Another story holds that one night in 1654, Pascal was seized by a mystical experience. When it ended he scribbled furiously on some parchment for nearly an hour in undecipherable handwriting. From that moment on he devoted himself to his religious studies, with few exceptions.

Pascal turned out to be as good a writer as he was a mathematician. From 1654 to 1658 he produced a series of pamphlets called *Provincial Letters,* which raised religious argumentation to a new literary height and was remarkably popular throughout France. At the time of his death he was preparing another book that would act as an apology (a formal defense) for the Christian faith, which dealt with every facet of Christian life and which was posthumously published as *Pensées,* or *Thoughts.*

Pascal did return to mathematics one last time in his adult life. He was suffering from a toothache and found himself thinking about the cycloid curve. Soon he noticed the toothache was gone. Taking this as a sign of divine approval, Pascal devoted a week to making discoveries about the cycloid. When he was done, he abandoned mathematics, never to take it up again.

At his death, the parchment from his mystic experience some twelve years earlier was found sewn into the lining of his shirt, close to his heart. What was Pascal's experience? We will never know. While Pascal's contributions to mathematics may have been brief, they were invaluable.

L'Hospital's rule for finding the limiting value of a fraction when the numerator and denominator both tend to zero is well known to calculus students. What they don't know is that L'Hospital did not discover the rule but obtained it from another mathematician in one of the best (or worst) business deals in all mathematics history.

The story begins with Johann Bernoulli (1667–1748), who was born on July 27, 1667, a member of the remarkable Swiss family that boasted of four generations of renowned mathematicians. Bernoulli was an able mathematician, one of the few to fully comprehend the new calculus.

Bernoulli was hired by French nobleman and amateur mathematician Marquis de L'Hospital (1661–1704) to tutor him in calculus. In a later agreement, L'Hospital hired Bernoulli to "work on what I shall ask you … and also to communicate to me your discoveries, with the request not to mention them to others." This agreement resulted in prominence and prosperity for L'Hospital and heartache for Bernoulli.

In 1696 L'Hospital organized the lessons and discoveries from Bernoulli into *Analyse des Infiniment Petits*, the first textbook printed on differential calculus. It was an immensely popular textbook which finally presented an elementary introduction to calculus. Although L'Hospital acknowledged Bernoulli in the preface, the material in the text was attributed to L'Hospital, including what is now known as L'Hospital's rule.

Bernoulli said nothing while L'Hospital lived, but when L'Hospital died in 1705, Bernoulli cried "Foul!" He spent the remainder of his life screaming plagiarism, but in vain. L'Hospital's book remained popular for years after his death. It was not until the twentieth century that Bernoulli's notes on differential calculus were discovered. They reveal that L'Hospital's rule was first developed by Bernoulli, several years prior to L'Hospital's publication. By virtue of his agreement with L'Hospital, Bernoulli forfeited fame and fortune for a yearly fee of a few dollars.

Picture a world-famous mathematician blinded at the height of his career. What could be expected of him in the remaining seventeen years of his life? Swiss mathematician Leonhard Euler (1707–1783) continued with an amazing output of work.

Euler was born in Basel, Switzerland, on April 15, 1707. After traditional schooling in which he did not distinguish himself, he entered the University of Basel to study for the ministry. While there, he had the good fortune to meet Johann Bernoulli and become friends with Bernoulli's two sons, Daniel and Nicolas, all mathematicians. The three Bernoullis convinced Euler to pursue mathematics.

In 1723 he obtained his master's degree in mathematics, and at age nineteen he won a prestigious prize for designing the best arrangement of masts on a sailing ship. Although Euler had never even seen a sailing ship, he used mathematics to logically design the winning entry. From Switzerland, Euler moved to Russia for a time, then to Germany.

Euler lost sight in one eye while still a young man. (Some contemporaries say it was from overwork in mathematics.) In 1766 he lost the sight in his remaining eye. Euler responded to the blow of becoming blind optimistically, stating, "I'll have fewer distractions!" How right he was.

Euler is the most prolific mathematician of all time. He wrote on topics such as engineering, topology, networks, mechanics, calculus, number theory, analysis, astronomy, optics, and geometry, to name just a few. The amount of his output is prodigious by any standards. His collected works amount to 886 books and pamphlets, which will total about seventy-four large volumes when they are all finally printed and catalogued. When he died, his obituary required fifty pages just to list all his publications. It is estimated that one-third of all the mathematics and scientific literature published in the eighteenth century came from his pen. Euler's major works are *Introductio in Analysin Infinitorum* (1748), *Institutiones Calculi Differentialis* (1755), and *Institutiones Calculi Integralis* (1768). Note that the latter work was published after he became blind.

Blindness never slowed down Euler. With the help of a formidable memory and two secretaries, he forged ahead. Euler memorized the first one hundred primes, as well as their squares, cubes, and fourth, fifth, and sixth powers. He intervened during a dispute between two of his secretaries and calculated the fiftieth place of an infinite series! Euler, it seems, could work under any condition. As a younger man he did most of his work at home, with thirteen children underfoot, or, more likely, a baby in one hand and a pen in the other. Blindness was simply another complication that Euler overcame in his pursuit of mathematics.

If you were born to a family of wealth, had all the advantages of the nobility, and were a regular member of the court of King Louis XV of France, would you ever think of mathematics? Émilie du Chatelet (1706–1749) had all of these advantages, yet she also became the first lady of French mathematics.

Du Chatelet was born on December 15, 1706, into a family that enjoyed all the privileges of life at the royal court in France. Her father was Louis Nicholas de Tonnelier, soon to become Baron de Breteuil, head of protocol at the court of Louis XV. French society at this time regarded women as intellectually inferior to men and so du Chatelet had to overcome major obstacles to achieve fame in mathematics.

Since her family was well stationed in life, du Chatelet had a private tutor, who awakened in her a love for learning and allowed her to develop her natural ability in mathematics. She was a brilliant child and had an extraordinary ability with numbers. French writer and philosopher Voltaire claimed he saw her find the product of two 9-digit numbers using only mental calculation.

In time, she became the constant companion of Voltaire, remaining with him until her death. It was Voltaire who urged her to put her mathematics to good use and write a much needed translation of Isaac Newton's *Principia*. She wrote such an outstanding translation of the *Principia* that to this day it is still the only French translation of Newton's masterwork. It was published posthumously in 1759 to great acclaim.

Imagine spending most of your adult life caring for your twenty younger brothers and sisters and doing humane works, only to be mistakenly associated with witchcraft. This is exactly what happened to Italian mathematician Maria Gaetana Agnesi (1718–1799).

Agnesi was born on May 16, 1718, near Bologna, Italy, the oldest child in a family that boasted twenty-one children. By all accounts, Agnesi was a child prodigy. By the time she was nine years old she had mastered five languages: Italian, Latin, Greek, French, and Hebrew. Her father, Pietro Agnesi, was a mathematics professor who took care to educate his children in all subjects, including mathematics.

Agnesi especially enjoyed mathematics and excelled in it. By age twenty she was publishing mathematics treatises. It is said that when she reached a difficult problem she could not solve, she would go to bed. During the night she would awaken and, in a sleeplike state, would write out the answer! In the morning she would awaken to find the completed solution on her writing desk with no memory of her nocturnal efforts.

In 1748, after ten years of work, Agnesi finally finished her great work *Analytical Institutions*. It was begun as a calculus text for her younger brothers and was a compendium of much of the mathematics known at that time. In her book Agnesi synthesized the calculus of Newton and Leibniz and also treated analytical geometry and algebra. The French Academy of Science called her book "the most complete and well-written of its kind." It was very popular and was translated into French and English.

In 1750 Agnesi was nominated to a full professorship at the University of Bologna by Pope Benedict XVI. There is some question as to whether she actually taught there as a professor, merely filled in for her father, or even ever set foot there. In any event, with the death of her father two years later, Agnesi gave up her mathematics and devoted the remainder of her life to caring for the rest of her brothers and sisters and working for charitable organizations.

Agnesi is known for creating the Curve of Agnesi, also known as the "Witch of Agnesi," a curve that can be formed using the following equation: $x^2y = 4a^2 (2a - y)$. The curve appears on the Cartesian plane as shown below.

The title "Witch of Agnesi" came about through a mistranslation of the term by which this cubic curve is known. For an unknown reason, Italian mathematician Guido Grandi (1671–1742) gave the curve the Latin name *versoria,* meaning "a rope which guides a sail." Agnesi, in her book of 1748, mixed up Grandi's word with the Latin word *versiera.* When English mathematician John Colson translated Agnesi's work on the versed sine, he mistranslated *versiera* (Latin "to turn") as the word *avversiera,* meaning "wife of the Devil." Since that translation, Agnesi has been identified with a witch, a remarkable twist of fate for a woman who devoted the last thirty-seven years of her life to charitable and religious works.

Could you build a full-size striking clock using only a knife and a borrowed pocket watch as a model? That's what Benjamin Bannekar (1731–1806) did when he was only twenty-two years old.

Bannekar was born in Maryland on November 9, 1731. His father was a slave who eventually bought his freedom, and his mother was a free African American. Bannekar was able to attend elementary school until he was old enough to work on his parent's farm. Each day after work, he read books to teach himself literature, history, and mathematics.

Bannekar was intensely curious, and made up for the lack of books at home by studying everything firsthand. Bannekar became famous in his Baltimore community for his ability to work with numbers and solve problems. Furthermore, he became an excellent farmer.

When Bannekar was in his forties, the Ellicott family, wealthy decedents of English nobility, moved into the area. Bannekar became friends with George Ellicott, an amateur mathematician and astronomer. Ellicott encouraged Bannekar's talents by lending him books and instruments on astronomy. Within months, Bannekar had mastered logarithms and was making astronomical computations. He even found errors in some of the famous scholarly works he read.

Bannekar soon came to national attention. In 1791, President Washington commissioned Andrew Ellicott and Pierre L'Enfant to lay out the new national capital of Washington, D.C., in a location on the Potomic River south of Baltimore. Andrew Ellicott, a cousin to George Ellicott, had heard about the remarkable Banneker and enlisted his help in the venture. It was a fortuitous decision. L'Enfant, after experiencing a number of personal difficulties with nearly everyone involved, including George Washington, eventually left his commission and took the plans for the capital city with him. Banneker was able to draw up a new set of plans from memory!

After returning from Washington, Bannekar, who was sixty years old, completed his first almanac. It was a summary of his astronomical calculations and detailed observations of the night sky. Bannekar sent of copy of it to Thomas Jefferson, who was so impressed with the manuscript that he sent it to the French Academy of Science. Bannekar published more than ten years' worth of almanacs that were so well done that they were distributed internationally by the anti-slavery movement as "proof that the powers of the mind are disconnected with the colour of the skin."

The clock Bannekar made at age twenty-two was just the beginning of Bannekar's success as a self-taught mathematician, astronomer, surveyor, and mechanic. To make the clock, Bannekar reportedly took apart and studied pieces of a pocket watch lent to him by a traveling merchant. Then he calculated the proper ratios of gears and wheels and with a knife carved all the parts out of wood.

Event of the Week

Imagine corresponding for several years with Karl Friedrich Gauss (1777–1855), the world's greatest mathematician, but concealing your identity with a pseudonym. Why was Sophie Germain (1776–1831) unwilling to use her real name? The reason is in the tenor of the times.

Born in Paris, France, on April 1, 1776, Sophie Germain grew up in difficult times, and was just entering her teenage years when the French Revolution struck France with all its fury. Also, her parents were staunchly opposed to her study of mathematics.

After the furor of the Revolution had passed, Germain applied for acceptance to the newly founded École Polytechnique, but even the Revolution did not change the status of women in education, and she was refused admission. Undaunted, she collected lecture notes from various students, sent homework assignments under a pseudonym to the great French mathematician Joseph Louis Lagrange (1736–1813), and continued with her mathematics.

After she wrote a number of published articles, her fame as a mathematician grew. In 1810 Napoleon Bonaparte ordered a prize for the best essay relating the mathematics laws of elastic surfaces to experimental data. After a few unsuccessful entries, Germain entered a paper, which won the grand prize from the French Academy in 1816. Her paper discussed the vibration of elastic surfaces, a topic that has been useful in the building of modern towers and skyscrapers with a steel superstructure.

After this success, Germain was admitted into the highest circles of French intellectual life and enjoyed her position as the successor to Émilie du Chatelet (1701–1749) as the foremost woman mathematician in Europe.

What about her correspondence with Gauss? As an undergraduate, Germain excelled in her studies and in 1804 sent a manuscript to the German mathematician commenting on an article he had published. Since she was an unknown student and a woman at that, she signed her name as M. LeBlanc, an actual student at the École Polytechnique. Germain continued to correspond with Gauss under the pseudonym M. LeBlanc until 1807, when French troops seized Hanover, Germany, the town where Gauss lived. Fearing for Gauss's safety, Germain contacted the general of the French troops, who was a relative, and asked that Gauss's safety be assured. The general looked after Gauss and revealed to him that Germain was the brilliant M. LeBlanc of the letters he had received from France. Although they never met, Gauss and Germain carried on a long correspondence with Germain signing her own name to letters from then on. Gauss was moved to write of Germain, "When a woman because of her sex, our customs and prejudices … overcomes these problems, she doubtless has the most noble courage, extraordinary talent, and superior genius."

Can one day in a person's life change his or her whole life's course? It happens. In the case of Karl Friedrich Gauss (1777–1855), it happened the day he solved a mathematics problem.

Gauss was born on April 30, 1777, in Brunswick, Germany. From the beginning he was a first-class genius, especially in mathematics. According to Gauss, he could "reckon" even before he could talk. At age three he was correcting payroll totals for his father, and by age ten the teachers at his school told his family they could teach him no more. Fortunately, word of the child prodigy reached the Duke of Brunswick, and he became Gauss's patron for the next twenty years. The Duke's support enabled Gauss to devote himself to his studies and research. The young Gauss was adept at the study of languages; by nineteen he had already mastered German, Greek, Latin, English, Danish, and French, and he added Russian and Swedish in later life.

On March 30, 1796, nineteen-year-old Gauss discovered how to construct a regular 17-sided polygon with a compass and straight edge. This was the first advancement in constructions since the time of Euclid, and the discovery so pleased Gauss that he decided to pursue mathematics rather than study languages. What a pursuit it was! Gauss made extensive contributions in the areas of geometry, differential geometry, statistics (the bell-shaped curve), probability, topology, magnetism, surfaces, crystalogy, optics, algebra (the fundamental theorem of algebra), and electricity, to name only some of the areas he researched.

Gauss himself felt the construction of a regular 17-sided polygon was an important event in his life. He left instructions for a regular 17-sided polygon to be put on his memorial stone. Today, there is a 17-point star (the stone cutter thought a 17-sided polygon would look too much like a circle) on Gauss's memorial stone, commemorating his discovery. Never has a student responded so well to the solution of a single problem!

It is always hard to be the first at anything. It takes something special to open the way for others to follow. Mary Fairfax Somerville (1780–1872) blazed a trail for women mathematicians at a time when women were deemed too frail for academic rigors.

Somerville, born on December 26, 1780, was the first woman mathematician of modern times in England. She grew up in a period when programs for female students did not exist at the university level, even for families as well connected as Somerville's. Women were schooled in a few areas, such as reading, writing, and a bit of arithmetic, but science and higher mathematics were out of the question.

When Somerville was ten, her father, Vice Admiral William Fairfax, returned from another of his long sea voyages to discover that his daughter was unruly and could barely read. He sent her to a girl's school for a short time, mainly to learn social graces, but also to be educated. Upon leaving the girl's school, Somerville was prepared to take her place in the role set out for women—domesticity. Instead she discovered mathematics, particularly algebra.

Ironically, Mary's interest in mathematics was sparked at a tea party. While flipping through a fashion magazine, her eye caught a page mixed with Xs and Ys. When asked what this was, her friend answered, "It's a kind of arithemetic; they call it Algebra." Somerville, unsatisfied with this answer, decided to investigate algebra more closely.

Once Somerville's interest was ignited, there was no holding her back. She secretly obtained a copy of Euclid's *Elements* from her brother's tutor and sat in on her brother's lessons. The tutor was so impressed with her ability that he supplied her with other mathematics books, which she quickly mastered.

When Somerville was twenty-seven years old, her husband of three years died. She decided to devote the rest of her life to studying mathematics.

Although Somerville published a number of articles and papers in her career, she is best remembered for an English translation of Pierre Laplace's *Méchanique Céleste*. In this masterwork of 1825, Laplace (1749–1827) presented a full discussion of the mathematics of contemporary astronomy. The mathematics was quite complex, and few of the problem sets had solutions. Somerville not only translated Laplace's book into understandable English, she also added explanatory comments and solutions to all of the problems. Her translation was published in 1831 to the acclaim of all England.

Mary Fairfax Somerville had broken the ice and cleared the way for future generations of women mathematicians in England. She was especially helpful to another woman mathematician of her time, Ada Lovelace (1815–1852). Somerville introduced Lovelace to Charles Babbage (1792-1871); together, Lovelace and Babbage would develop the mathematics for modern computers.

During the years of the French Revolution, when the common people rebelled against the French monarchy, everyone who was even remotely connected with royalty was in danger. Even surveyors working for the Revolution to establish the new metric system came close to meeting death at the guillotine.

On June 22, 1799, the metric system was adopted as the official system of weights and measures by the French National Assembly. However, the beginnings of the metric system go back more than two hundred years earlier.

In 1585 Simon Stevin (1548–1620) published *La Disme,* in which he advocated decimal fractions as well as a system of measurements based on a decimal system. The cause of a metric system was next taken up in 1670 by Gabriel Mouton, Vicar of St. Paul's Church in Lyon, France. He advocated a decimal measurement system, and suggested that the unit of measure be derived from one minute of a degree of the length of a longitude line.

The matter lay dormant until the French Revolution of 1789, at which time France had over 800 units of measure. (A *tois,* for example, was a unit of length approximately 1.95 meters long.) As part of the revision of laws, customs, and society in general, the subject of a new system of measurement was introduced to the French National Assembly by Charles Talleyrand (1754–1838), a renowned French diplomat. On August 19, 1791, the proposal for the new system was presented to King Louis XVI, one day before his futile attempt to escape from France. He gave his enthusiastic approval to the idea, but it is questionable whether he paid much attention to the presentation, with his planned escape only hours away.

In any event, the National Assembly directed the French Academy of Sciences to develop a new system of measures that would be derived from the measurement of a longitude line. Accordingly, a group of mathematicians, accountants, and scientists was assembled for the task, including the mathematician Adrien Legendre (1752–1833). The group decided to use as its basic unit one ten-millionth of the meridian length from the North Pole to the equator through Paris. This unit of length was called a "meter," and was derived from the Greek word *metron,* meaning "to measure." The meridian's length was to be determined by finding the distance from Dunkirk, France, to Barcelona, Spain. This task, which would have been difficult under ideal conditions, took six years to complete because of frequent wars and changes in government and personnel.

Finally, the metric system was presented to the French government, along with a platinum rod a meter long and a platinum bar weighing a kilogram. The metric system became the official measuring system of France, accompanied by the motto, "For all the people, for all time."

Old ways die hard, however, and in 1811 Pierre Laplace (1749–1827) proposed calling the system "Napoleonic measures" so as to ensure its use and the emperor's support. By 1840 the metric system became accepted throughout all of France and in other countries where it was carried by Napoleon's troops. Today, only the United States and one or two other countries use any other system.

Why didn't the United States whole-heartedly adopt the metric system? Some sources blame the pirates who roamed the Atlantic Ocean two hundred years ago. As the story goes, the French National Assembly sent a representative bearing a kilogram and a meter to the United States with news of their new measurement system. The representative's ship was attacked by pirates, sunk, and the representative was enslaved, never to deliver the metric system to colonial America.

How did the surveyors working on the metric system come close to a tragic end? The sighting crews on the survey teams used white sighting cloths for lining up their instruments. This got them into big trouble, because white was the color of royalist supporters. The surveyors avoided the guillotine when new sighting cloths using the politically correct colors of blue, red, and white—the colors of the revolution—replaced the white sighting cloths.

What would you do if you knew you were going to die in the morning and had only one night left to live? If you were Évariste Galois (1811–1832), you would spend the night feverishly doing mathematics!

Galois, the son of a small town mayor in France, was born on October 25, 1811, at the height of Napoleon's reign. Soon, Napoleon would be out of power and a succession of governments would try to rule France. It was the changes in government that spelled doom for Galois.

Galois was a brilliant student but also an impatient one. He was sarcastic in class and did not assume the subservient role held by the students of his day. One story of his youth claims he hurled chalk and erasers at the examiner for entrance to the Ecole Polytechnique because the man was too slow to comprehend his new mathematics, abstract algebra.

In 1831, Galois served a brief prison term for having spoken out in opposition to the king. Although he was released, he was a marked man, considered a potential opponent to the regime of Louis XVIII. In addition, Galois continued to be abrasive to everyone he met. Consequently, the local military determined to be rid of him. The plot was simple. A local woman would play up to Galois, and when he returned her attention, the captain of the guard would claim Galois had offended his lady's honor. A duel would be demanded, and Galois's fate would be sealed. Events went exactly as planned.

On the evening before the duel, May 29, 1832, Galois began to annotate his notebooks, write personal letters, and put to paper all of his mathematical discoveries. What he wrote was new to mathematics and involved topics that have only been explored in the past century. Galois initiated the mathematics of abstract algebra and the study of group theory.

At dawn, he went out to meet his fate. He was shot and fell, mortally wounded. Hours later a passing peasant assisted him to a physician's house, but it was too late for Galois, and he died the next morning. His name lives on because of his ground-breaking work, written on the eve of his fatal duel. It is because of those few hours of writing that Galois has a place in mathematics history. Who knows what Galois might have achieved had he recovered to live a normal life span?

How does a person rise above the lowest class of society to become a college professor of mathematics? The life of George Boole (1815–1864) presents us with just such a dramatic achievement.

George Boole was born on November 2, 1815, in Lincoln, England, to a lower class family. Boole received the education typical for the times: minimal elementary school training with a bit of mathematics and Latin thrown in for good measure. Boole's father, a common laborer who quit school in the third grade, also tutored Boole, giving his son the benefit of his life experience in mathematics.

Boole felt that he was destined for better things, so he worked hard to improve his prospects. In Boole's view, a knowledge of Latin and Greek were likely keys to moving up in life, so he began to teach himself both languages. At age twelve, he entered a public contest for Latin scholars, and while he was commended for his efforts, there was some criticism of his ability. The result was that Boole redoubled his efforts.

When Boole was sixteen, he found employment as an assistant in an elementary school in order to improve his family's financial situation. The family finances continued to decline, and by the time Boole reached twenty, his parents were totally dependent on him. Boole opened his own elementary school, teaching the students what he had taught himself in mathematics, foreign languages, and writing. He also published his first mathematics paper on the topic of invariants.

This paper caught the attention of a number of mathematicians, but Boole resisted all offers of appointments to other positions because of his responsibility to support his parents. In 1848 he published a pamphlet entitled *Mathematical Analysis of Logic, Being an Essay Towards a Calculus of Deductive Reasoning*. This was so well received that he was offered a professorship at Queen's College in Cork, Ireland. He accepted the position and was finally at a point where finances were no longer a concern. Boole had risen to the level of society to which he felt destined.

Boole was now able to improve and expand on the ideas in his pamphlet. In 1854 he published *An Investigation of the Laws of Thought, on Which are Founded the Mathematical Theories of Logic and Probability,* a work that constitutes a dramatic departure from all algebra preceding it. In this masterwork, Boole reduced the study of logic to algebra and developed the reasoning required for programming computers a century later.

In 1855 Boole married Mary Everest and was finally content. His happiness lasted only nine years. One day Boole walked to a lecture in a cold rainstorm and insisted on giving his presentation in his wet clothes. He caught a chill, which developed into a fatal pneumonia.

Boole's life was one of hard work and perseverance to attain a goal. Boole recalled that at age seventeen, while walking through a field, a thought "flashed upon him" from out of nowhere. His work later in life evolved from that flash of insight, which told Boole that humans derive knowledge from some undefinable, invisible source besides books and teachers.

What reward should be given to a professor who invented a whole new branch of mathematics, gave forty years of faithful service to his university, oversaw the rebuilding of classrooms, organized and expanded the library, and acted as provost to the entire student population? Nicolai Lobachevsky (1793–1856) did these things and more for the University of Kazan, in Russia.

Lobachevsky was the son of a Russian laborer. His father died when he was three, and his mother moved with her three sons to Kazan, near Siberia. She taught the boys at home until they reached the age for elementary school. All three won scholarships to local schools.

Lobachevsky was an especially adept student. He started school when he was eight years old and at age thirteen entered the University of Kazan, a newly formed institution. He received his master's degree at age eighteen and became a teacher at Kazan, becoming a full professor ten years later and a rector at age thirty-three. In addition to his teaching duties, he was chief librarian and headed the construction and refurbishing of university buildings. He also oversaw the observatory and ran the museum.

These services alone should have earned him the gratitude of the university, but Lobachevsky achieved even more. He broke new ground in mathematics. On February 23, 1826, Lobachevsky delivered a paper, *A Brief Statement of the Elements of Geometry with a Rigorous Proof of the Theorem on Parallels,* which dealt with his conclusions about a new geometry he called "imaginary geometry," an unfortunate choice of words. In his paper he presented a polished version of the geometry he had envisioned for a textbook as early as 1823. The textbook was never published because it used the metric system brought about by the French Revolution, and the Russians had had quite enough of the French during Napoleon's recent invasions. In any event, his non-Euclidean geometry was met with general indifference by the faculty.

Determined to make his new geometry known, Lobachevsky published *On the Foundations of Geometry* in the *Kazan Messenger* three years later.

Since the article was written in Russian, and Kazan was on the edge of nowhere, it was largely ignored. Lobachevsky persisted in publicizing his work and sent a copy of his ideas to the St. Petersberg Academy of Science. Again, his work was ignored.

In 1840 he translated a new book, *Geometrical Investigation on the Theory of Parallels,* into French and German and sent an updated copy to Karl Friedrich Gauss (1777–1855) for approval. While Gauss approved of the young mathematician's ideas, he responded, "You know that for fifty-four years I have held the same convictions. I have found nothing that is new to me." It appears Gauss had reached the same conclusions in the privacy of his notebooks. Although he agreed with Lobachevsky's work, he gave no public support to Lobachevsky, and so Lobachevsky had to struggle alone to make his work known.

During all this Lobachevsky continued his administrative and teaching duties at the university. He succeeded in pulling the university up to a level of academic esteem in Russia. His services appeared to have been in vain, however. In 1846 Lobachevsky was summarily dismissed from the university in the belief that he had stayed long enough and had reached the mandatory retirement age.

After his dismissal from the university, Lobachevsky kept trying to gain recognition for his ideas. He received some awards and honors but was still largely unknown, even within the greater mathematics community. In 1855, blind and in failing health, Lobachevsky dictated a newer version of his geometry in the hope that it would finally be well received. It was too late. He died the next year, unhonored at home for his service and unhonored abroad for his mathematics.

In modern times, Lobachevsky has been recognized as the "Father of non-Euclidean Geometry." He has posthumously been awarded mathematics prizes and stamps and has even had a geometry named after him. What a pity he never lived to enjoy these honors.

Although the electronic computers were first built in the 1940s, two essential components of every computer program were discovered a century earlier by Ada Lovelace (1815-1852).

Lovelace is known as the first computer programmer. In spite of the fact that she suffered poor health and faced opposition from her family, Lovelace succeeded in making discoveries in mathematics that had far-reaching effects on modern computer programming.

Lovelace was the daughter of Annabella Millband and poet Lord Byron. She never really knew her famous father, who left the family shortly after her birth, never to return. Lovelace was raised by her mother's family and received the standard education of the time for young women: reading and writing, with very little science and mathematics. As a result, she was essentially self-educated in mathematics, devoting herself so much to it that a family friend, George Gorden, called her "Princess of the Parallelogram."

At age nineteen Lovelace married Lord William King, who became Earl of Lovelace three years later. In spite of her husband's disapproval, a growing family, and deteriorating health, she continued her studies of mathematics. As a result of her mathematics ability, she was introduced to Mary Fairfax Somerville (1780–1872), the "first lady of British mathematics." This led to a second introduction, which was to have profound consequences for the history of mathematics.

In 1833, Somerville introduced Lovelace to Charles Babbage (1792–1871), the mathematician who had built the difference engine, a calculating machine that ran on steam power. This outstanding mathematician soon became Lovelace's tutor. In a short time, Lovelace became his assistant and then his collaborator.

Babbage's newest idea was an analytical engine capable of very involved calculations, including calculus. Lovelace's role was to provide the programming logic for such a machine. It was Lovelace who suggested using the binary system of 0's and 1's for calculations. More significant, she conceived the idea of a subroutine with a loop, that is, a portion of a program that would perform repeated calculations as needed. Both concepts are fundamental to the development of modern computers.

Unfortunately for Babbage, the mechanical precision required for his analytical engine was beyond the technology of his time and it was never built. (An analytical engine was built in 1991; it performed exactly as Lovelace and Babbage predicted.) As for Lovelace, her health continued to fail, and she died of cancer at the young age of thirty-nine. Lovelace and Babbage never saw the reality of their visions, but their accomplishments have earned both of them a place in the history of mathematics and the history of computers.

In all the history of mathematics, few mathematicians have ever had to overcome the opposition to studying mathematics that Sonya Kovalevsky (1850–1891) did. Her story is all the more poignant because of its sudden, sad end.

Kovalevsky was born on January 15, 1850, to an aristocratic family in czarist Russia. Her father was a general in the Russian army, and her grandfather and great-grandfather were well-known mathematicians. She was raised by an English nanny who also tutored her, so she received more of an education than the typical young girl of her time. Her nanny had awakened in her an unquenchable thirst for knowledge, especially in mathematics.

Advanced education for women was unheard of at this time in Russia. When she was eighteen years old, Kovalevsky decided to marry and move to Heidelberg, Germany, where she was able to attend university classes.

When Kovalevsky's husband committed suicide in 1883, she went to Berlin to study with the great mathematician Karl Weierstrass (1815–1897) at the University of Göttingen. The university did not accept women, so Weierstrass kindly became Kovalevsky's tutor and patron, sharing his lecture notes with her for the next four years. In 1874, although still not accepted as a student, Kovalevsky was awarded a Ph.D. in mathematics from Göttingen.

Even with her degree, Kovalevsky was unable to find a position at any university. Finally, Swedish mathematician Gosta Mittag-Leffler (1846–1927) obtained a professorship for her at the University of Stockholm in 1883. During her career, Kovalevsky wrote remarkable papers on partial differential equations and infinite series. She also made important contributions to astronomy, including mathematically describing the egg-shaped rings of Saturn.

In 1888 Kovalevsky won the *Prix Bordin* from the French Academy of Sciences. Her topic was "On the Problem of the Rotation of a Solid Body about a Fixed Point," and her essay was so well written that the normal prize of three thousand francs was increased to five thousand francs "on account of the service rendered to mathematical physics by this work."

By this point Kovalevsky was well known throughout Europe and the following year she became the first woman member of the Russian Academy of Science. Her success was to be short-lived, however; she died suddenly of influenza a year later. One can only imagine what was lost to the world of mathematics by her early death.

Emmy Noether (1882–1935) was born on March 22, 1882, in Erlangen, a small university town in southern Germany. She is considered by many to be the finest woman mathematician who ever lived. Even Albert Einstein (1879–1955) considered her to be his superior in mathematics.

Noether's father, Max Noether, was himself a well-known mathematician, and it is from him that she received encouragement and tutoring in mathematics. Noether was a natural in mathematics but found it difficult to progress to the university level. In 1898 she applied for admission to the University at Erlangen but was denied entrance by the Academic Senate for fear that admitting a woman would "overthrow all academic order." For a time she was tutored by a family friend, Paul Gorden, who was a mathematics professor. In 1900 she was finally allowed to attend lectures, and four years later she was permitted to enroll. She received her Ph.D. in mathematics on December 13, 1907.

Even with her degree in hand, Noether found much resistance to the idea of a woman mathematician. For a number of years she lectured for her father at the university, since she herself was not permitted to fill a faculty position. During these years she also began to publish a variety of articles dealing with abstract algebra, her specialty. She moved on to the University of Göttingen, where she worked with the great mathematician David Hilbert (1862–1943) on the general theory of relativity. Noether and Hilbert worked out a system so she could give lectures that were announced under his name, which she did for three years without pay. In 1926 she was appointed a full professor, but still received no salary. Finally, three years later and through Hilbert's efforts, Noether was accepted at a salaried position.

In 1933, the National Socialist party came to power in Germany. Since Noether was a Jew, she felt it best to leave her homeland. She settled in the United States at Bryn Mawr College, where she was a popular teacher who "talked fast and wrote even faster" during her lectures.

Noether is primarily known for work in abstract algebra and a theorem which is said to be the cornerstone of general relativity. She was well liked by students and colleagues alike, even though her lectures were given at such breakneck speed it was difficult for all but the expert to keep up. She died suddenly in 1935 after a routine operation.

It is the rare student who has not wished at least once that math was easier and calculations were not so tedious. On February 11, 1897, an attempt was made to create simpler mathematics. A bill was presented to the Indiana state senate to change the value of π to a value such as $3\frac{1}{5}$.

The value of π has been a source of mathematics research from the beginning of recorded history. As early as 1700 B.C. the Egyptians used the equation $A = (d - \frac{1}{9}d)^2$ to determine the area of a circle. Such a formula results in a value of 3.16 for π, a remarkably accurate value for the time. Some fifteen hundred years later, Archimedes found the value of π to lie between $3\frac{1}{7}$ and $3\frac{10}{71}$. In the fifth century, Chinese mathematician Tsu Ch'ung-Chih found the simple fraction that renders the closest approximation of π: $\frac{355}{113}$), or about 3.14159292. This fraction differs from π by only about three ten-millionths.

With the development of the calculus, the value of π was determined to be irrational, and mathematicians discovered a number of infinite series that could be used to calculate π. For example, Gottfried Wilhelm von Leibniz (1646–1716) found that $\pi = 4(1 - \frac{1}{3} + \frac{1}{5} - \frac{1}{7} + \frac{1}{9} \ldots)$, and Leonhard Euler (1707–1783) found $\pi^2 = 6(\frac{1}{1^2} + \frac{1}{2^2} + \frac{1}{3^2} + \ldots)$. Series such as these led to even more exact values for π. In 1610, for example, Ludolph van Ceulen (1540–1610) calculated the value of π to thirty-five decimal places.

In modern times, William Shanks (1812–1882) published the value of π to 707 places, a task to which he devoted fifteen years of his life. It was not until the age of computers that his work was checked. In 1948 an error was found in the 528th place! Recently, David and Gregory Chudnovsky have used a super computer to calculate π to 1,011,196,696 decimal places.

What was the outcome of Indiana's attempt to legislate mathematics? Fortunately, there were some mathematically literate senators in session that day, and the bill was defeated.

On rare occasions a mathematics term can be traced to a specific event or a particular day. On still rarer occasions, the term becomes commonly accepted into the vocabulary of everyday speech. Grace Murray Hopper (1906–1992) coined such a term.

In the words below, Hopper describes an incident that occurred in 1945 when she was working with two colleagues on the Mark I, the world's first large-scale digital computer.

> Things were going badly. There was something wrong with one of the circuits of the long glass-enclosed computer. Finally we located the trouble spot, and using ordinary tweezers, removed the problem, a two-inch moth. From then on, when anything went wrong with the computer, we said it had a bug in it.

Thus originated the term *bug* for any glitch in a computer program. The term bug has since been generalized and is used commonly in expressions such as "Get all the bugs out."

The most famous moth in mathematics may be seen today in a museum in Newport News, Virginia. It is in the same place that Hopper and her colleagues dutifully taped it, next to the entry in the log book for 1545 hours, September 9, 1945.

Historical
Problems

1: Magic Squares

Magic squares are the most popular recreation in mathematics. The first magic square appeared in the *Book of Permutation*, written in China in about 2200 B.C. Legend has it that Emperor Ta-Yu conceived the first magic square after seeing a turtle with an odd pattern on its shell. Since that time magic squares have been part of the mathematics of nearly every culture. Albert Durer, a German painter of the sixteenth century, included a magic square in his painting "Melancolia," and United States founding father Benjamin Franklin wrote extensively about them and amused himself with them "to avoid Wear-iness" while he was a clerk in the Pennsylvania assembly.

A magic square consists of numbers arranged in a square so that all rows, columns, and usually the two diagonals will add up to the same sum. Try to create a magic square by arranging the first nine counting numbers in the nine square cells below. There is only one possible arrangement.

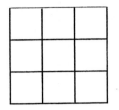

The greater the number of cells in a magic square, the more possible solutions there are. To complete the magic square started below, arrange the remaining twelve of the first sixteen counting numbers in the empty cells.

16			
	10		
		7	
			1

2: The Möbius Band

August Möbius (1790–1868) is well known for his discoveries in the field of topology, which is the study of surfaces. The Möbius band is named after him. Möbius was an astronomer by occupation and began to develop his ideas on topology and the Möbius band at the advanced age of sixty-eight. The Möbius Band has many unusual properties that you will explore in this set of exercises.

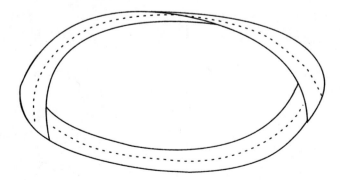

Follow these steps to create a Möbius band:

1. Cut a strip of paper 1 inch wide and about 10 inches long.

2. Twist one end a full 180 degrees and tape it to the other end. It should look something like the following diagram.

Now try the following exercises with your Möbius band:

1. Draw a line down the middle of the Möbius band. Continue until the line meets itself. What do you notice?

2. Use a pair of scissors to cut the Möbius band along the line you drew. What happens?

3. Make another Möbius band and draw a line that is one third of the width from an edge. Continue the line until it meets itself. Now cut along that line. What happens?

3: Star Polygons

French mathematician Louis Poinsot (PWAN so) (1777–1859) made contributions to the mathematics of the Solar System, the theory of numbers, and geometry. He is also known for his beautiful patterns on a circle, which he called star polygons. The star polygon below is drawn on a circle that is divided into eight equal arcs. Every other arc point is connected to form the pattern. Poinsot designated this pattern (8, 2), meaning eight arc points, with every second point joined.

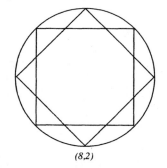

(8,2)

Try a different star polygon in the circle below. Use a pattern of (8, 3), that is, join every third point of the eight arc points shown here.

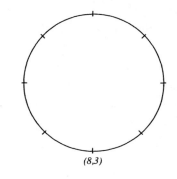

(8,3)

Can you find any other patterns that make star polygons?

4: Boole Cards

Mary Everest Boole (1832–1916) was married to Irish mathematician George Boole (1815–1864). She popularized one recreational form of mathematics known as Boole cards. Follow the directions below to create a Boole card.

Using straight lines, connect points with matching numbers—that is, connect point 1 on the vertical ray to point 1 on the horizontal ray.

1. What shape do these straight lines form?

2. What happens to your shape if the rays form a different angle (other than 90 degrees)? Try a few different angles to find out.

3. What happens when the points on one ray are spaced differently than those on the other ray? What happens if the points are not evenly spaced on either one of the two rays? Try a few spacing varieties to find out.

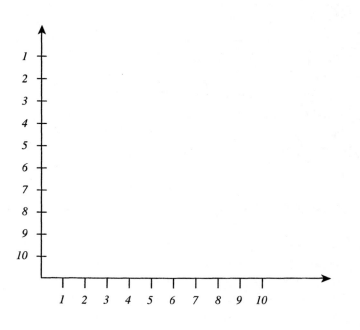

5: The Wolf, the Goat, and the Cabbage

Alcuin of York (735–780) collected a number of problems based on fables from the Dark Ages and published them in a book entitled *Problems for the Quickening of the Mind*. One of the problems, the problem of the wolf, the goat, and the cabbage, is very popular and has reappeared in mathematics literature since at least the year 700. It is paraphrased here—try to solve it.

Make a series of diagrams to help explain how the ferryman could get everything safely across the river.

A wolf, a goat, and a cabbage must cross a river in a boat that can hold only one passenger besides the ferryman. How must the ferryman carry them across so that the goat is not left alone with the cabbage and the wolf is not left alone with the goat?

6: The Sieve of Eratosthenes

Eratosthenes (c. 276–194 B.C.) was a Greek mathematician born in a Greek colony west of Egypt. He was more than a mathematician, and he wrote on subjects such as geography, astronomy, poetry, and history. For his many talents, he was called Pentathlos, meaning "All-Around One" by his admirers. His critics called him Beta, meaning "second-rate," because they felt that although he did outstanding work in everything he tried, none of it was truly superior.

Eratosthenes is known for his sieve, a method used to discover prime numbers. A prime number is an integer other than 1 that has no factors but itself and 1. Seven is a prime number, while six is not $(2 \times 3 = 6)$. The sieve of Eratosthenes can be used to "sift out" all the prime numbers in the list below. Circle the first prime number, 2, and then cross out all numbers that are multiples of 2. (This has already been done.) Circle the next prime number, 3, and then cross out all multiples of 3: 6, 9, 12, and so on. Continue circling prime numbers and crossing out their multiples until every number is either circled or crossed out. All the circled numbers are prime numbers.

②	3	~~4~~	5
~~6~~	7	~~8~~	9	~~10~~
11	~~12~~	13	~~14~~	15
~~16~~	17	~~18~~	19	~~20~~
21	~~22~~	23	~~24~~	25

7: Lewis Carroll's Doublets

In 1879 Lewis Carroll, the author of *Alice in Wonderland* and professor of logic at Oxford University, sent in a new type of puzzle he called a doublet to *Vanity Fair* magazine. He thought up these puzzles when two young girls told him they had nothing to do. The girls liked these puzzles so much that Carroll showed them to friends, who also thought they were fun to solve. The object of a doublet is to change one word to another through a series of steps in which only one letter may be changed at a time. Each change must form a new word. For example, one of Carroll's doublets was to change PIG into STY.

PIG ....PIT .....PAT ....SAT ....SAY ....STY

Try solving the following doublets:

1. CAT into DOG

2. CAR into JET

3. COOL into BELT

Make up a few doublets of your own and try them out on a classmate.

8: Needle in a π Stack

Georges Louis Leclerc, the Compte de Buffon (1707–1788), was an aristocrat who pursued mathematics as a recreation. He is famous for translating Isaac Newton's calculus books into French and for the following problem/activity that results in a value of π (3.1416). Follow the directions below to duplicate Buffon's experiment.

1. Cover a piece of paper with horizontal, parallel lines that are 1 inch apart.

2. Drop a 1-inch long piece of uncooked spaghetti onto this lined paper.

3. Record whether or not the piece of spaghetti comes to rest on a line.

4. Repeat this process for 25 tosses and keep track of the results.

5. Determine the following value:

$$2\left(\frac{\text{Tries}}{\text{Hits}}\right) =$$

According to Buffon (and later verified by the French Academy of Science), the greater the number of tosses, the closer the value will be to π. How close did you come?

9: The Inventor of Chess

There is a legend (dating from around the seventh century) that King Shirhan of India wanted to reward the inventor of chess, mathematician Grand Vizier Sissa Ben Dahir. The king decided to grant Sissa anything he wished. Sissa asked for a chessboard to be brought out. Pointing to the chessboard, Sissa asked that it be filled with grains of wheat in the following manner: one grain on the first square, two on the second, four on the third, eight on the fourth and so on, doubling the number of grains from one square to the next for all sixty-four squares. The king was astounded at so humble a request, but agreed to grant it.

Did Sissa ask too little? Suppose Sissa had asked for pennies rather than grains of wheat. If you were king, would you have granted his request? Use the chessboard below to figure out how much money would be on square 20 alone (use a calculator):

1	2	3	4	5	6	7	8
9	10	11	12	13	14	15	16
17	18	19	20	21	22	23	24
25	26	27	28	29	30	31	32
33	34	35	36	37	38	39	40
41	42	43	44	45	46	47	48
49	50	51	52	53	54	55	56
57	58	59	60	61	62	63	64

How much money would be on square 30?

10: The Fibonacci Sequence

In 1202 the Italian mathematician Fibonacci (c. 1175 –1250), wrote a book entitled *Liber Abaci*. It was the first book published in Europe which used our modern number system. All previous books had used Roman numerals. *Liber Abaci* contained what has become known as the rabbit problem. The problem reads as follows:

A man put a pair of rabbits in a certain place entirely surrounded by a wall. How many pairs of rabbits will be produced from that pair in a year, if the nature of these rabbits is such that each month each pair bears a new pair which from the second month onward become productive?

To solve the problem, make a chart to show the number of rabbits in each month, and look for a pattern. The pattern that solves the problem has also been applied to architectural design and great works of art. Solve Fibonacci's problem by extending the chart below.

				Total Pairs
Jan. 1		PAIR 1		1
Feb. 1		PAIR 1 —— pair 2		2
Mar. 1	pair 3 —— PAIR 1	PAIR 2		3

11: As I Was Going to St. Ives

This problem, like many others, appears in the mathematics literature of nearly every culture. The English version of this problem is in the form of an old nursery rhyme you may have heard.

As I was going to St. Ives
I met a man with seven wives;
Every wife had seven sacks;
Every sack had seven cats;
Every cat had seven kits (kittens).
Kits, cats, sacks, wives,
How many were going to St. Ives?

How many were going to St. Ives?

12: "There It Lies"

Karl F. Gauss (1777–1855) is one of history's greatest mathematicians. Young Gauss (gowse) showed his promise in mathematics at an early age. When Karl was only three, he was sitting on a stool watching his father working on the payroll for his small brickyard. At the end of one of the computations, Karl announced to his father that he'd made an error. Mr. Gauss checked his work and discovered that his young son was right. From then on, Mr. Gauss had Karl check all his work.

Another telling event took place when Karl was ten years old. On the first day of class, Karl's teacher, Mr. Buttner, told the pupils to sum the numbers from 1 to 100 to keep them busy while he tended to administrative duties. In those days students did their work on slates and placed the slate flat on their desk when they were finished. According to the story, Karl took ten seconds to think about the problem before he wrote a solution on the slate and placed it in his desk, declaring "There it lies." The rest of the class toiled for the remainder of the hour. At the end of the class period, Mr. Buttner discovered that Karl was the only one who found the correct solution.

Can you find the sum of the numbers 1 to 100 as quickly as Karl did? He did it without adding them up one at a time as his classmates tried to do. Look for number patterns to shorten your work.

13: The Circumference of the Earth

At the time of Columbus's voyage to the Americas, it was a well-known fact that the earth was round. Only peasants still believed a ship could sail off the end of the earth. The ancient Greeks were well aware that the earth was round. One of them, Eratosthenes (air ah TOSS the neez) (c. 276–194 B.C.), figured out the circumference of the earth. How did he do it?

Eratosthenes heard about an unusual well in Syene, Egypt, which was located 5000 stadia ("stadiums") directly south of his city of Alexandria. On the longest day of the year, this deep well reflected the sun on the surface of water at its bottom, meaning the sun was directly overhead at that time. Eratosthenes knew that at the same time in Alexandria, a vertical rod cast a shadow. By imagining that the hypotenuse of a right triangle extended from the tip of the rod to the tip of the shadow, Eratosthenes found that the angle at the tip of the rod was 7 degrees. This angle is congruent to the angle of separation between the two cities as shown in the diagram below.

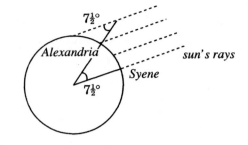

With this information he was able to calculate the earth's circumference. Can you recreate his calculations? Determine the earth's circumference in miles. One stadium is equal to 500 feet. There are 5,280 feet in one mile.

14: The Formulas of Heron and Brahmagupta

The typical formula for the area of a triangle is $A = \frac{1}{2}bh$. How can the area of a triangle be determined when its altitude is unknown but the lengths of its three sides are known? Heron of Alexandria (c. 75) found a method to determine the area of a triangle given only the lengths of its three sides. His formula is $\sqrt{s(s-a)(s-b)(s-c)}$ where a, b, and c represent the lengths of the sides and s represents one-half the perimeter.

Using this formula, find the area of the following triangle if $a = 8$, $b = 18$, and $c = 14$.

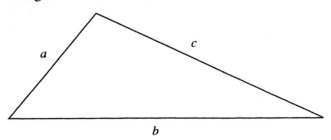

A related formula for cyclic quadrilaterals (quadrilaterals that can be inscribed in a circle) was discovered by the great Hindu mathematician Brahmagupta (c. 628). His formula is $\sqrt{(s-a)(s-b)(s-c)(s-d)}$ where a, b, c, and d represent the lengths of the sides of the quadrilateral, and s represents one-half the perimeter.

Find the area of the cyclic quadrilateral below if $a = 12$, $b = 6$, $c = 9$, and $d = 7$.

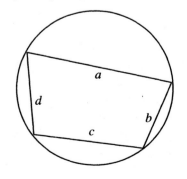

136

15: Al-Khwarizmi's Will

There is a legend about the will of one of the greatest Arab mathematicians who ever lived, al-Khwarizmi. Around the year 800, Al-Khwarizmi lived in what is now Iran and wrote about arithmetic and algebra. The word *algebra* is derived from the Arab word *al-jabr,* which he used in the title of one of his books. Al-Khwarizmi was the first Arab mathematician to write about the new concept of zero. His books were also the first Arabic books to be translated into Latin.

Al-Khwarizmi's will was drawn up when he was near death and his wife was expecting their first child. In his will al-Khwarizmi stipulated that if his wife were to have a son, the son would inherit two thirds of his estate, and his wife the remaining one third. If his wife had a daughter, however, then his wife would inherit two thirds of his estate, and the daughter one third. As it turned out, shortly after al-Khwarizmi's death his wife had twins—a boy and a girl. The legend does not explain how the inheritance was finally divided, but you may be sure that al-Khwarizmi's wishes were followed. How should the inheritance have been divided among his wife, his son, and his daughter so that al-Khwarizmi's wishes were respected?

16: The Life of Diophantus

Diophantus of Alexandria (c. 275) was an outstanding Greek mathematician who wrote extensively on quadratic equations. He also collected and catalogued all of the algebra the Greeks had achieved. Nothing is really known about his life, when or where he lived, or how he died. All that is known about him comes from an algebra problem, written about Diophantus and inscribed on his tombstone.

The problem is as follows:

Diophantus passed $\frac{1}{6}$ of his life in childhood, $\frac{1}{12}$ in youth, and $\frac{1}{7}$ more as a bachelor, five years after his marriage was born a son who died four years before his father at half the age at which his father died.

Can you figure out Diophantus' age when he died?

17: America's Greatest Puzzlers

Sam Lloyd has been called America's greatest puzzler. He was born in 1844, and after an undistinguished education he began to create puzzles. The puzzles were so original and appealing that soon his problems were appearing in newspapers and magazines all over the country. Eventually his collection of puzzles numbered over five thousand. Here is one of his puzzle problems.

> A man had accumulated a large ball of string. The ball was two feet in diameter and represented 15 years of collecting string. The average diameter of the string he saved was $\frac{3}{8}$) inch. How long was the string?

The mantle of America's greatest puzzler passed from Sam Lloyd to Martin Gardner, who was an editor for *Scientific American* for many years and published many recreational mathematics books. Below is one of his problems.

A ten-volume encyclopedia stands on a shelf, as shown. Each volume is 2 inches thick. Suppose a bookworm starts at the front cover of Volume 1 and eats his way in a straight horizontal line through to the back cover of Volume 10. How far does the worm travel?

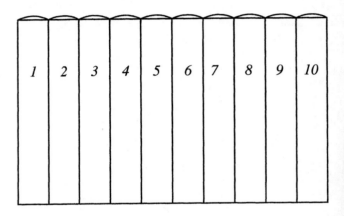

18: Euler's Formula

Can you solve these puzzle problems?
Leonhard Euler (1707–1783) discovered a remarkable relationship between the various parts of any polyhedron (a solid figure with many faces) such as those pictured below. Euler (OY ler) found that adding the number of vertices (such as point A in Figure 1) to the number of faces (such as rectangle ABCD) and subtracting the number of edges (such as segment AB) resulted in the same number regardless of the type of polyhedron. Fill in the chart below and complete Euler's equation.

Polyhedron	Vertices + Faces – Edges = ?
Rectangular Solid	
Triangular Pyramid	
Square Pyramid	

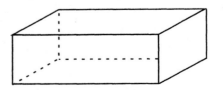

Rectangular Solid

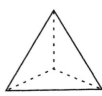

Triangular Pyramid

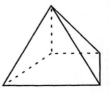

Square Pyramid

19: *Pons Asinorum*

This Latin name was given to Proposition 5, contained in Book I of Euclid's *Elements*. It states:

> In an isosceles triangle [such as *ABC*] the angles at the base [∠*ABC* and ∠*ACB*] are equal to one another, and, if the equal straight lines be produced further [*BD* and *CF*], the angles under the base [∠*DBC* and ∠*FCB*] will be equal to one another.

Prove Proposition 5 using the diagram below.

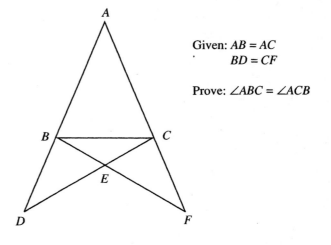

Given: *AB* = *AC*
        BD = *CF*

Prove: ∠*ABC* = ∠*ACB*

20: Branchion's Claim to Fame

Charles Julien Branchion (1785–1864) made his biggest contribution to mathematics while he was still a student at the Polytechnical School in Paris. Although he later collaborated with Jean Victor Poncelet on the nine-point circle, Branchion was only twenty-one when he discovered the following theorem:

> If a hexagon is circumscribed about a conic section, then the three diagonals which join opposite vertices are concurrent (meet at one point).

Verify Branchion's theorem by making a drawing as directed below.

1. Circumscribe an irregular hexagon (a figure having six straight sides and six angles) *ABCDEF* about a conic section (either a circle, ellipse or parabola).
2. Draw diagonals *AD*, *BE*, and *FC*.
3. Do they meet at one point?

21: The Shortest Proof in Geometry

Below is the shortest proof of the Pythagorean theorem, which states that $a^2 + b^2 = c^2$. This one-word proof was written by the Hindu mathematician Bhaskara (1114–1185).

Here is an identical diagram with the sides of the right triangle labeled to help you recreate his proof. Cut up this diagram and rearrange it to prove $a^2 + b^2 = c^2$.

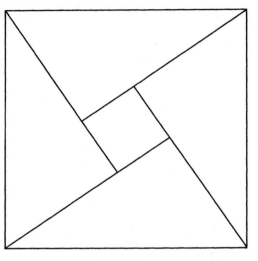

BEHOLD

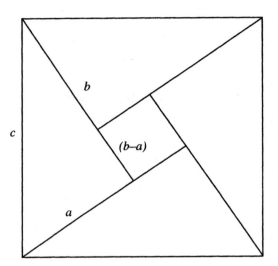

22: The Simson Line

In one of the great injustices in mathematics history, a discovery made in 1797 by William Wallace (1768–1843) has been attributed to another mathematician, Robert Simson (1687–1768). The discovery, now known as Simson's line, describes a construction and states: *If a triangle is inscribed in a circle, the feet of the perpendiculars drawn from any random point on the circle to the sides of the triangle are collinear.*

Construct Simson's line below by following the directions.

1. Construct a circle and inscribe triangle *ABC*.
2. Select random point *P* on the circle.
3. Construct perpendicular *PX* to meet side *AB*, perpendicular *PY* to meet side *BC*, and perpendicular *PZ* to meet side *AC*.
4. Draw the line that contains points *X*, *Y*, and *Z*. This is Simson's line.

23: The Nine-Point Circle

Karl Wilhelm Feurbach (1800–1834) first discovered and proved the existence of the nine-point circle in a short work published in 1822. Charles Julien Branchion (1785–1864) and Jean Victor Poncelet (PON se lay) (1788–1867) also discovered the nine-point circle working together in 1820–1821, but the theorem has been linked to Feurbach.

Follow the directions below to construct the nine-point circle:

1. Draw a triangle QRS.
2. Construct the midpoints of the three sides and label them A, B, and C, respectively.
3. Construct the altitudes from vertices Q, R, and S to sides SR, QS, and QR and label the points of intersection D, E, and F respectively.
4. Label the orthocenter (the point where the three altitudes constructed in step 3 meet) and label it point O.
5. Draw segments from point O to the points A, B, and C.
6. Find the midpoints of OQ, OR, and OS and label them G, H, and I, respectively.
7. The nine-point circle passes through points A, B, C, D, E, F, G, H, and I.

24: Fermat's Point

Pierre de Fermat (1601–1665) was a lawyer and civil servant for the French government who dabbled in mathematics in his spare time. He never published any of his discoveries but did correspond with nearly all of the great European mathematicians of his time. For a while, Fermat was the clearinghouse for all mathematical progress in Europe. In response to a problem he received, Fermat determined the location of a minimum point in a triangle. A minimum point is the point that is the shortest total distance to all three vertices. In the map below, if a company wanted to set up a central office that was the shortest total distance from the three towns, it would be located at what is called Fermat's point.

• Knoware

• Infinity

Follow these directions to construct Fermat's point.

1. Draw any random triangle ABC with no angle greater than 120 degrees.
2. Construct equilateral triangle ABQ on side AB, equilateral triangle BCR on side BC, and equilateral triangle CAS on side CA.
3. Draw segments QC, RA, and SB. They will meet at point F, which is Fermat's point. If point F is located at Fermat's point, then $FA + FB + FC$ will be less than the total distance of the segments drawn from any other point in the triangle to its three vertices.

• Eureka

4

History of
Mathematical Symbols

1 Origin of the + and − Signs

The first occurrence of the two signs is in *Behennde unnd hubsche Rechnug auff Kauffmanschafften* (1489) by German mathematician Johann Widmann (1462–1498). Of note, however, is a series of notes from 1481, annotated by Widman, which contain the same symbols. Could Widman have copied these symbols from some unknown professor at the University of Leipzig? It is uncertain. What is known for certain is that a student's notes from one of Widmann's 1486 lectures show the + and − signs. There is an object lesson here, teachers: Make sure that your name appears in your students' notes.

2 Origin of the < and > Signs

English mathematician Thomas Harriot (1560–1621) first used these symbols in *Artis Analyticae Praxis* ("Practice of the Analytic Art"), posthumously published in 1631. Harriot was commissioned in 1585 by Sir Walter Raleigh to survey North America. While there Harriot saw a Native American with this symbol on his arm: ⋈
It is likely he developed the > ("greater than") and < ("less than") symbols from this symbol. Unfortunately for Harriot, he also developed a habit of using tobacco in the form of snuff while in the Americas. He died of a cancerous ulcer of the left nostril, the first recorded case of death due to the use of tobacco.

3 Origin of the = Sign

In 1557 Robert Recorde (c. 1510–1558) first used the = symbol in *The Whetstone of Witte*, the first algebra book written in English. He explained his choice of a symbol to represent "equals" as follows: "I will sette as I doe often in work use, a paire of paralleles or Gemowe lines of one length, thus: ═══ bicause noe 2 thynges can be moare equalle [*sic*]." As noted, Recorde used an elongated form of the present symbol. The term *gemowe* marked an unsuccessful attempt by Recorde to coin a new

mathematics term. *Gemowe* is an arcane English word meaning "twin." An interesting postscript is that the equal sign did not appear in print again until 1631, when was used in texts by Thomas Harriot (1560–1621) and William Oughtred (1574–1660).

4 Origin of the Symbols × and • for Multiplication

Englishman William Oughtred (1574–1660) incorporated the symbol × for multiplication along with as many as 150 different symbols, some new and some borrowed from other mathematicians, in his masterwork *Clavis Mathematicae*, published in 1631.

In the same year Thomas Harriot's book *Artis Analyticae Praxis* was published, and in it Harriot appears to use a raised dot (•) as a symbol for multiplication. Some believe, however, that Harriot was simply separating a coefficient from a variable (6 • y), rather than showing multiplication. In 1698 Gottfried Wilhelm von Leibniz (1646–1716) explains in a letter that he used an interposed (raised) dot to indicate multiplication. Both multiplication symbols survive to this day.

5 Origin of the Symbols ° for Degrees, ' for Minutes, and " for Seconds

These symbols were all introduced by Claudius Ptolemy (c. 85–c. 165), the famous Greek mathematician, in his masterwork, *Almagest* (from an Arabic word meaning "greatest"). Ptolemy most likely used a circle to represent degrees, since the measure of an angle is based on the 360° circle. The symbol is also related to the form of the Greek letter *omicron*.

Besides introducing the ' and " symbols, Ptolemy also coined the terms *minutes* and *seconds* to designate the subdivisions of a degree. He divided the degree into smaller parts, which he called *pars minutae prima,* or "first division of parts." The term *minute* is derived from this designation. Ptolemy described the further division of a minute into smaller parts as *pars minutae secundae* or "secondary division," which led to the term *seconds*.

Some mathematics historians suggest that the practice of dividing a circle into 360 parts originated with the Babylonians and their mistaken notion of a 360-day year. The Babylonians also used only sexagesimal fractions (fractions with sixty as the denominator), which Ptolemy adopted for his *Algamest*. Arab mathematician Kushyar Ibn Labban (971–1029) used the term *degree* to refer to integers, *minute* to refer to fractions of the type $\frac{x}{60}$, and *second* to refer to even smaller fractions of the type $\frac{x}{60^2}$.

The use of ° to represent degrees was popularized in modern times in a book written by Dutch mathematician Gemma Frisius (1508–1555), published posthumously in 1569. The degree symbol appears in the book's appendix, which was written by a little-known French mathematician named Jacques Peletier (1517–1582) who wrote also a number of algebra and geometry texts.

6 Use of Raised Numerals for Powers

French philosopher and mathematician René Descartes (1596–1650) first used the modern notation for powers. In his book *La Géométrie,* published in 1637, Descartes improved on the efforts of two earlier mathematicians to notate exponents clearly. In 1636 James Hume, a Scotsman living in Paris, suggested rendering $8b^4$ as $8b^{IV}$, using Roman numerals instead of Arabic numerals to designate the exponent. In *Cursus Mathematicus,* published in 1634, Frenchman Pierre Herigone suggested writing $8b^4$ as $8b4$ with no raising of the exponent. In this instance, Descartes' notation of $8b^4$ proved to be the best. A final note: Although Descartes invented modern notation for powers, he continued to write xx and not x^2. In this he was supported by many mathematicians on the grounds that xx occupies the same amount of space on a line of type as does x^2, and allows the type to be set on the same line.

7 Origin of the Symbols < and ∠ for Angle

French mathematician Pierre Herigone first used < to designate "angle" in his book *Cursus Mathematicus* (1634). Herigone used a great many new symbols in this six-volume work. He felt these symbols enabled him to "make demonstrations, brief and intelligible, without the use of any language." In 1657 William Oughtred (1574–1660), vicar of Shalford and rector of Albury, used ∠ in *Trigonometria,* thus popularizing a symbol for angle that could be distinguished from the "less than" symbol.

8 Use of *x* for an Unknown

The use of symbols for unknown values began with the Egyptians and continued throughout history in mathematics writings, with various symbols and combinations of letters being used according to the preference of the writer and the intended audience. François Viète (1540–1603) was the first mathematician to systematize the use of letters for unknowns. In his scheme, vowels represented unknown quantities and consonants, known values.

Within a few decades, however, René Descartes (1596–1650), in his book *La Géométrie* (1637), advocated using the first letters in the alphabet for known values, and the last letters in the alphabet for unknown values. The equation $ax + by = c$ introduced by Descartes is still used to describe the equation of a line.

The predominant use of the letter x to represent an unknown value came about in an intersting way. During the printing of *La Géométrie* and its appendix, *Discours de La Méthode,* which introduced coordinate geometry, the printer reached a dilemma. While the text was being typeset, the printer began to run short of the last letters of the alphabet. He asked Descartes if it mattered whether *x, y,* or *z* was used in each of the book's many equations.

Descartes replied that it made no difference which of the three letters was used to designate an unknown quantity. The printer selected x for most of the unknowns, since the letters y and z are used in the French language more frequently than is x.

9 Origin of the Symbol ∴

The symbol that still designates "therefore" in logic was first published in *Teusche Algebra* by Swiss mathematician Johann Rahn (1622 –1676). This was also one of the first mathematics texts published in Europe to make use of Robert Recorde's symbol for equal $=$.

10 Origin of Calculus Notations

The development of the calculus involves two of the greatest minds in mathematics: Sir Isaac Newton (1642–1727) and Gottfried Wilhelm von Leibniz (1646–1716). While Newton was perhaps the greatest mathematician in history, Leibniz was nearly his equal in mathematics. Leibniz was also a jurist, philosopher, and theologian.

During his great intellectual outpouring in the years 1664 to 1666, Newton developed a method of "fluxions" (rates of change) which he used in his theories of infinite series, calculus, optics, and gravitation. In the notation for his calculus, Newton used $\dot{x}$ for dx. Newton did not publish his findings, a habit that prompted Augustus DeMorgan to comment, "Every discovery of Newton had two aspects. Newton had to make it and then you had to find out that he had done so."

In contrast to Newton, Leibniz freely published all his findings. He also developed a different approach to the calculus, which he revealed in a series of letters and articles beginning in 1677. In these articles he progressively refined his notation until he reached the expression $\int_o^x dx$, still used to denote the infinite integral, a sum that measures the exact area under a curve. There is some evidence that Leibniz adopted the infinite integral symbol

because it resembles the letter s, the first letter in the word *sum*. Leibniz also used $\frac{dx}{dt}$, in contrast to Newton's notation $\dot{x}$.

Considering the clumsy writing instruments of the day, Newton's notation was far more difficult to write and read.

Leibniz published his complete calculus findings in an article that appeared in *Acta Eruditorum,* published in 1685. Since Newton had not published his calculus (he finally did so in an appendix to his 1704 book, *Opticks*), Leibniz was hailed as the inventor of calculus and was the toast of Europe. Only when news of Leibniz's publication of the calculus reached him did Newton reveal his earlier development of it. This set off a controversy which was to have drastic effects on British mathematics. Since the British mathematicians naturally sided with Newton's claim of having invented the calculus (actually, both men independently developed different approaches to the subject), they doggedly held to Newton's method and his poor notation. This devotion to Newton's notation paralyzed British mathematics until the early nineteenth century when Charles Babbage (1792–1871) of computer fame led the adoption of "Leibniz' *D*-ism" and the rejection of "Newton's Dotage." Those who stubbornly clung to Newton's notation were said to be in their "dotage."

11 Origin of the Symbol π

Leonhard Euler (1707–1784) is generally credited for popularizing the symbol for pi in a book published in 1737. However, π first appeared as a lone symbol for the circumference-diameter ratio in the 1706 work *Synopsis Palmariorium Matheseos,* by English mathematician William Jones (1675–1749). Included in Jones' book was a hundred-place value for π calculated by John Machin (1680–1751). William Oughtred (1574–1660) had previously used π to represent the circumference of a circle but did not use it to represent the circumference-diameter ratio, as did Jones. It is believed that Jones chose π to represent the circumference-diameter ratio because it is the first letter in the Greek word *perimetron,* meaning "the measure around the perimeter."

12 Origin of the Radical Sign

The first use of the radical sign as we recognize it was by German mathematician Christoff Rudolff (c. 1500–c. 1547) in *Behend unnd Hubsch durch die kunstreichen reglen Algebre so gemeincklich die Coss genent werden,* published in 1525. Some earlier texts use a dot and a "tail" on the dot that extends upward to the right. It is believed that this combination of dot and tail is meant to represent a form of the letter *r,* the first letter in the Latin word for *root.* The dot-with-a-tail symbol was not as striking as Rudolff's symbol, $\sqrt{}$. French mathematician René Descartes (1596–1650) added the bar to Rudolff's radical sign in his masterwork, *La Géométrie,* published in 1637, thus producing the radical sign we use today, $\sqrt{}$.

13 Origin of the Σ Symbol

Leonhard Euler (1707–1783) was the first to use the summation symbol. Euler published an astonishing amount of mathematical literature on nearly every conceivable topic. Today his collected works fill seventy-five volumes, and that does not include the more than five-thousand letters he wrote. Euler's amazing output of work was achieved while working almost exclusively in a home filled with thirteen children and several household pets!

14 Use of Parentheses in Mathematics

One of the first to consistently use parentheses to set apart portions of mathematical expressions was Christopher Clavius (1537–1612), a Jesuit friend of Johannes Kepler (1571–1630). Clavius was the chief mathematician behind Pope Gregory XIII's revision of the Julian calendar. He wrote on arithmetic and algebra topics. French mathematician François Viète (1540–1603) first used parentheses in *Zeletica,* published in 1593. Viéte was also the first to use letters of the alphabet for unknown quantities.

15 Origin of the Decimal Point

Flemish mathematician Simon Stevin (1548–1620) first used decimal fractions in his work *La Disme,* published in 1585, but he utilized a circle rather than a decimal point. The word *dime* is derived from the title of Stevin's book. Some believe that Stevin adopted decimal fractions from the Chinese, since he is known to have described "sailing wagons" which were in use in China at the time. Christopher Clavius (1537–1612) first used a decimal point for decimal fractions in 1593 in a table of sines.

16 Origin of the Horizontal Fraction Bar (for example, $\frac{1}{2}$)

The first European mathematician to use the fraction bar as it is used today was Leonard of Pisa (c. 1175–1250), better known by his nickname, Fibonacci. He published a mathematics text in 1202 that showed the influence of his merchant travels through Mediterranean lands. In his text, Fibonacci used Hindu-Arabic numerals, the first Western European to do so. Fibonacci most likely derived the idea for a fraction bar from Arabic mathematicians as well, possibly from al-Hassar, who lived in the twelfth century.

17 Origin of the : Symbol to Indicate a Ratio of Two Integers

Gottfried Wilhelm Leibniz (1646–1716) is credited with being the first to use this symbol. He included it in an article he wrote for *Acta Eruditorum* in 1684.

18 Origin of the :: Symbol to Show Proportion

William Oughtred (1574–1660) first used the double colon to show proportion in his seminal work, *Clavis Mathematicae,* published in 1631. His full demonstration of a proportion using the double colon (*a.b:c.d*) was still not what is used today. It remained for an astronomer, Vincent Wing, to be the first to write a proportion in the same form as it is written today. In *Harmonicon Celeste,* published in 1651, Wing expressed a proportion as *a:b::c:d.*

19 Origin of the Solidus Symbol as a Fraction Bar (/)

The first appearance of the solidus symbol in fractions is in the writings of a Spanish mathematician from Mexico. As early as 1748, Manuel Antonio Valdes used a curved line, much like an integral symbol on a slant, in his book *Gazetasde Mexico.* It remained for another Spanish mathematician to straighten out the solidus to create the familiar *a/b* fractional expression used today. Antonio y Oliveres first began to use the straight solidus in 1852, and it has been a popular alternative to the fraction bar since it allows type to be set on the same line rather than on three different lines, as in the case of the traditional fraction bar.

20 Origin of the ‖ Symbol to Mean Parallel

William Oughtred (1574–1660) is the originator of the symbol for parallel that has survived to the present. He first used the symbol in *Opuscula Mathematica Hactenus Inedita,* which was published posthumously in 1677. Oughtred was also the inventor of the circular slide rule.

21 Origin of the ⌒ Symbol to Represent an Arc

This is one of the oldest symbols for which a specific originator is known. While many symbols that resemble geometric shapes have been in use since the time of the ancient Greeks, many cannot be attributed to a single mathematician. The symbol for an arc is first found in Plato of Tivolio's translation of *Liber Embardorum* by Savasorda, a Hebrew scholar who lived in Barcelona in about 1100.

22 Origin of the ~ Symbol

Gottfried Wilhelm Leibniz (1646–1716) receives credit for first using this symbol for similarity. It appears in an article he published in 1679. An editor used the same symbol, but backwards (⌐), in 1710, when referring to Leibniz's symbol. It appears Leibniz used these two symbols interchangeably.

23 Origin of the Symbol for Absolute Value

This symbol was first used by Karl Weierstrass (1815–1897) in 1841, when he represented the absolute value of the complex number $a + bi$ as $|a + bi|$.

24 Origin of the Infinity Symbol (∞)

This symbol was first used by John Wallis (1616–1703), a student of William Outghtred and the foremost English mathematician before Newton. Wallis introduced the ∞ symbol, possibly derived from the old Roman symbol for a thousand, in *Arithmetic Infinitorum* (1655). Wallis's writings dealt with infinitesimals as a precursor to calculus. He used $\frac{1}{\infty}$ to represent an infinitely small value. Wallis is also known for his infinite series:
$$4\left(\tfrac{2}{3}, \tfrac{4}{3}, \tfrac{4}{5}, \tfrac{6}{5}, \tfrac{6}{7}, \ldots\right) = \pi.$$

On December 22, 1669, Wallis, awake in his bed and unable to sleep, found the square root of 3,000,000,000,000,000,000,000,000, 000,000,000,000,000 by mental calculation!

25 Use of the [ ] Symbols

Brackets were first used in 1550 by Raphael Bombelli (1526–1573) in his *Algebra,* which discussed the roots of cubic equations. Bombelli was one of a group of outstanding Italian algebraists in the sixteenth century. He formulated the four basic operations with complex numbers and utilized continued fractions to find square and cube roots.

26 Origin of the % Symbol

This Symbol probably evolved from an anonymous Italian manuscript in 1475. In the manuscript the writer used P$\stackrel{o}{\subset}$, rather than "per 100" or "P 100" or even "P *centro,*" which were popular at the time. Eventually, by 1650, P$\stackrel{o}{\subset}$ became 8 so that *per* 8 was then in vogue. Finally, *per* was dropped and 8 was left to become the % of today.

27 Origin of the ! Symbol for Factorial

French mathematician Christian Kramp (1760–1826) of Strasbourg introduced this notation for factorial in *Elements d'Arithmetique Universelle,* published in 1808. He invented the new symbol as an improvement over existing symbols for factorial, which were more difficult to typeset.

28 Origin of the *i* Symbol for $\sqrt{-1}$

This first appeared in Leonhard Euler's (1707–1783) memoirs, published in 1794. Euler was blind for many of his last years, but that did not retard his work. He simply dictated his mathematics, calculations and all, to a secretary who recorded his ideas for publication.

29 Origin of the *e* Symbol

Leonhard Euler (1707–1783) first used *e* as the base of the natural system of logarithms in a letter written in 1731. In 1737 Euler proved that *e* is irrational (that is, it cannot be expressed as the quotient of two integers), and in 1873 the French mathematician Charles Hermite (1822–1901) proved that *e* is a transcendental number (that is, it cannot be expressed as the root of a polynomial equation with rational coefficients).

30 Origin of the Φ Symbol for the Golden Ratio

American mathematician Mark Barr chose this symbol for the golden ratio. The Greek letter φ is the first letter in the name of the sculptor Phidias (490–430 B.C.), who designed the Parthenon temple in Athens and the thirty-eight-foot tall statue of Athena that it contained. The statue was made of ivory and gold and was the masterpiece of his career. His name is linked to the golden ratio because the Parthenon displays the golden rectangle in so much of its design.

31 Origin of the ± Symbol

Englishman William Oughtred (1574–1660) incorporated this symbol in his masterwork, *Clavis Mathematicae,* published in 1631. Besides being known for introducing so many new symbols to mathematics, Oughtred was the first to use a straight logarithmic slide rule.

32 Origin of the ≃ Symbol for Congruence

Gottfried Wilhelm Leibniz (1646–1716) originated the symbol for congruence, which resembles our symbol today with some recent modification. Not all of Leibniz's symbols were universally adopted. He felt that the colon (:) was preferable to both the fraction bar and the ÷ symbol to indicate division.

33 Origin of the ⊥ Symbol for Perpendicular

French mathematician Pierre Herigone first used the ⊥ symbol for perpendicular in his book *Cursus Mathematicus* (1634). Herigone introduced so many new symbols in this six-volume work that some suggest that the introduction of these symbols, rather than an effective mathematics text, was his goal.

34 Origin of the Expression $f(x)$ for Function

This expression was first used by Leonhard Euler (1707–1783), who invented or popularized many symbols. Euler was perhaps the most prolific mathematics writer of all times. He wrote about calculus, topology, networks, and many other topics. It is Euler who used the seven key numbers and symbols of mathematics in a single expression: $e^{i\pi} + 1 = 0$.

35 Origin of the ≡ Symbol for Congruence

Karl Friedrich Gauss (1777–1855) first used the ≡ symbol in *Disquisitions Arithmeticae* (1801) to demonstrate congruence in number theory. In a modular system of base 3, $10 \equiv 1$. Gauss achieved discoveries in so many branches of mathematics that he is known as the "Prince of Mathematicians."

36 Origin of the ÷ Symbol

This symbol was first used by Swiss mathematician Johann Rahn (1624–1656) in *Teusche Algebra* (1659). In this book Rahn included an appendix that included the prime factors of all numbers up to 24,000 that were not divisible by 2 or 5. As impressive as this seems, J.P. Kulik (1773–1863) did even better: he devoted twenty years of his life to compiling a list of the factors of numbers up to 100,000,000!

37 Origin of the $ Symbol

In seventeenth-century Mexico, the symbol for the peso was P^s. This symbol was adopted by colonial America for the dollar, and evolved by stages to the familiar $. The $ symbol first appeared in print in 1717.

38 Origin of the # Symbol

The Latin phrase *libra ponds,* meaning "according to weight" or "properly weighed," was abbreviated by lb. Eventually lb was written in cursive and embellished with a final cross stroke: *℔*. In time this symbol became the # symbol used today.

History of
Mathematical Terms

Abacus: Taken from the Hebrew word *abhaq*, meaning "dust." This term is derived from the earliest mathematical table, literally a drawing board covered with dust on which calculations were made.

Abscissa: Taken from the Latin term *abscissus*, meaning "cut off line." The term *ordinate* is taken from the Latin term *ordinare*, meaning "to put in order." In combination these two terms make some sense. The ordinate is similar to a number line, putting numbers in order, while the abscissa is a line that cuts off the ordinate.

Absolute Value: This term was coined by Karl Weierstrass (1815–1897) who used the original meaning of the Latin term *absolvere*, meaning "to free from." The process of absolute value frees a number from its sign.

Acre: Taken from an Old English word *aecer*, meaning "field." In Olde England the term *field* was used to describe a plot of land suitable for cultivation.

Acute: Taken from the Latin word *acutus*, meaning "sharp." The term is still used to describe a sharp pain. The shape of an acute angle resembles a sharp knife, in contrast to a "dull" angle of 90 degrees (*see* Figure 1).

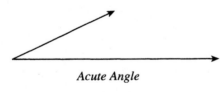

Acute Angle

Figure 1

Addition: Taken from the Latin word *addere*, meaning "to put together." Addition is the process of putting numbers together to find their sum.

Algebra: Derived from the Arabic word *al-jabr*, which appeared in the title of a book written in Baghdad about the year 825. The title of the text was *Hisab al-jabr w' al-muqabalah*, which loosely translated means "the science of reunion and reduction." It was written by the mathematician al-Khwarizmi. It was this book of algebraic equations that introduced Hindu-Arabic numbers, including zero, to Western Europe. The word *jabr* means "bone setting," hence the title of the text dealing with the "reunion" of equations, or the "setting of equations which had been broken." As a young man, al-Khwarizmi was sent as ambassador to Khazaria for a few years. This city lay on the major trade routes between the Middle East and India and China. Some believe he learned about the concept of zero there.

Algorithm: The term *algorithm* is derived from the name of the great Islamic mathematician al-Khwarizmi and is a corruption of his name translated into Latin. In *The Book of Addition and Subtraction According to the Hindu Calculation* (c. 825), al-Khwarizmi introduced the Hindu decimal positional system and the ten symbols for the Hindu-Arabic numerals to the Arab world. When translated into Latin, the Hindu system was introduced to Western Europe. A Latin translation of this book began, "Spoken has Algoritmi …."

Apothem: Taken from the Greek term *apothema*, meaning "away from a position." An apothem is the perpendicular distance from the center of a regular polygon to a side, in other words, the segment that is drawn "away from" the center "position" (*see* Figure 2).

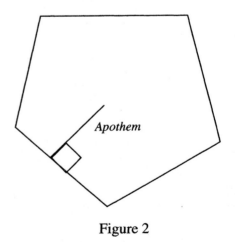

Apothem

Figure 2

Area: Taken from the Latin word *area*, meaning flat, open field. The concept of area was first used in land measurement.

Arithmetic: Taken from the Greek word *arithmetike*, meaning "the art of counting."

Asymptote: Taken from the Greek word *asumptotos,* meaning "not falling together." An asymptote never meets the curve of the hyperbola which approaches it.

Average: Taken from the Arabic term *awariyah ,* meaning "damaged goods." The loss to merchants due to damaged goods during shipping was equally shared, or averaged, among the investors.

Axiom: Taken from the Greek word *axioma,* meaning "that which is thought fitting." An axiom was a statement of obvious fact, accepted without proof.

Billion: Taken from the French words *bi* and *million,* meaning "two millions." Nicholas Chuquet, a fifteenth-century French mathematician, established the names for billion, trillion, quadrillion, and subsequent powers of ten. In *Triparty en la Sciences de la Nombres* (1484) he wrote, "The first dot indicates million, the second dot billion, the third dot trillion, the fourth dot quadrillion … and so on as far one may wish to go."

Calculus: Taken from the Latin word *calculus,* meaning "small stone." In early times small stones were placed in grooves drawn in the earth and then used much as beads are in an abacus.

Cevian: A cevian is a segment that joins the vertex of a triangle to a point on the opposite side (*see* Figure 3). This term is derived from the name of the mathematician who wrote about cevians, Italian mathematician Giovanni Ceva (1648–1734). It is one of the few mathematical terms derived from the name of a mathematician.

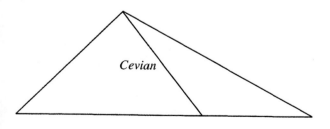

Figure 3

Characteristic: See mantissa.

Chord: Taken from the Latin term *chorda,* which was derived from the term for "bow string." The chord of a circle resembles a bow string in appearance (*see* Figure 4).

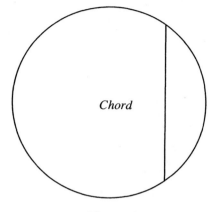

Chord

Figure 4

Circumference: Taken from the Latin word *circumferre,* meaning "to carry around." Derived from a Greek word meaning "boundary line." It was first used by Euclid (c. 300 B.C.) in *The Elements.*

Coefficient: Taken from the Latin terms *co* and *efficiens,* meaning "to effect together." A coefficient is "effected together" with a variable to produce a new value.

Commutative: Taken from the Latin word *commutare,* meaning "to exchange." The commutative property of addition or multiplication allows for exchanging positions of numbers without changing the value of the expression (for example, 3 + 4 = 4 + 3).

Compute: Taken from the Latin word *computare,* meaning "a notched tally stick." In ancient Rome a tally stick was used for calculations.

Concave: Taken from the Latin word *concavus,* meaning "vaulted or hollow." A concave figure may be considered to be "hollow" in extreme examples as shown here (*see* Figure 5).

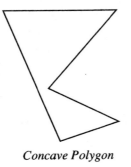

Concave Polygon
Figure 5

Concentric: Taken from the Greek words *con* meaning "same," and *centrom,* meaning "center." An interesting aspect of this word is its similarity to *eccentric,* which literally means "to be off center, out of normal."

Cone: Taken from the Greek term *konos,* meaning "sharp, pointed object." Apollonius of Perga (262–190 B.C.) matched this term to the shape in his book *Conic Sections.*

Congruent: Taken from the Latin word *congruens,* meaning "to meet together." Congruent figures are identical figures which, if placed one atop the other, "meet together."

Converse: Taken from the Latin term *conversus,* meaning "to turn around." The converse of any conditional sentence is derived by turning around the hypothesis and conclusion to form a new conditional.

Corollary: Taken from the Latin term *corolla,* meaning "a small garland." The term is thought to derive from the fact that since a corollary is based on a theorem, it need not be independently proven. A corollary is like a small garland that surrounds a more majestic flower, the original theorem.

Cylinder: Taken from the Greek word *kolindros,* meaning "roller." Anyone who has used a rolling pin can appreciate the origin of this term, first used in Apollonius of Perga's (262-190 B.C.) *Conic Sections.*

Degree: Taken from the Latin word *degradus,* meaning "to step down or away from." Evidently, the idea of a degree as a small measure of a circle is preserved in the Latin term: One steps down or away from a starting point of measurement.

Denominator: *See* Numerator.

Derivative: Taken from the Latin *de,* meaning "of," and *rivus,* meaning "stream." The term *derivative* came fairly late to the vocabulary of calculus. It was first used by Joseph Lagrange (1736–1813) more than a hundred years after calculus was invented. Isaac Newton (1642–1727), a coinventor of calculus, used the term *fluxions* when describing his method of calculus. His term never caught on.

Diagonal: Taken from the Greek terms *dia,* meaning "across" and *gonia,* meaning "angle." A diagonal is a segment, drawn across a polygon, which joins the vertices of two nonconsecutive angles (*see* Figure 6).

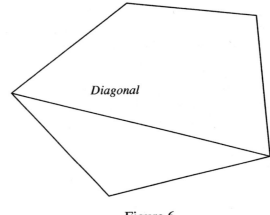

Diagonal

Figure 6

Diameter: Taken from the Greek word *diametros,* meaning "line which measures through." The ancient Greeks considered a diameter to be the part of a line that passes through the center of a circle. Its measure could be used to find the circumference and the area of the circle.

Digit: Taken from the Latin term *digitus,* meaning "finger." From earliest times fingers were used for calculations.

Dihedral: Taken from the Greek words *di,* meaning "two" and *hedral,* meaning "seat or base." The Greeks thought of a dihedral angle as an angle formed by two seats or bases.

Division: Taken from the Latin words *dis,* meaning "apart" and *ferre* meaning "to carry away." Division is the process of carrying away a part of the number that is being divided.

Ellipse: *See* Parabola.

Exponent: Taken from the Latin term *exponere,* meaning "to expound." The base of an expression with an exponent is expounded upon by the exponent.

Fathom: Taken from a Middle English term, *fadme,* which means the distance a man can "fathom" with outstretched arms. A sailor would determine the depth of the water by the number of times the anchor's rope reached across his outstretched arms.

Fibonacci Sequence: The series 1,1,2,3,5,8,13, … was named for Leonardo of Pisa (c. 1175–1250), whose nickname was Fibonacci. It was not until several hundred years after Fibonacci published a problem with a solution containing this famous sequence that his name was attached to it.

Foot: Taken from the Middle English word *fut,* meaning "foot." From Roman times the human foot was used as a rough estimate of length. An attempt to standardize the length of the foot was made in 798 when King Charlemagne of the Frankish Empire (which covered what is now France, Germany, and Italy) decreed that his royal foot would be the standard length in his realm. It was not to be. Several centuries later the length of a foot was standardized in England.

Fractal: This is a new term in mathematics, coined by Benoit Mandlebrot in an article entitled "Intermittent Turbulence and Fractal Dimension," published in 1976. The term *fractal* is derived from the Latin word *fractus,* which has the corresponding verb *frangere,* meaning "to break into irregular fragments." According to Mandlebrot, "It is sensible that in addition to 'fragmented,'… [fractal] should also mean 'irregular.'"

Fraction: This term was originated by English writer Geoffrey Chaucer (1342–1400) of *Canterbury Tales* fame. It has the meaning of a "broken number" in Middle English, and is derived from the Latin term *fractus,* meaning "to break." The Arabic word for fraction, *al-kasr,* is related to an Arabic verb that also has the meaning "to break."

Function: Taken from the Latin term *functio,* meaning "to perform." In mathematics a function is related to the performance of an operation. It was originated by Wilhelm Gottfried von Leibniz (1646–1716).

Geometry: Taken from the Greek word *geometrein,* meaning "to measure the land," no doubt derived from the first practical uses of geometry, land measurement.

Googol: This term, which refers to a number consisting of the number one followed by a hundred zeroes, or 10^{100}, was coined by the nine-year-old nephew of Dr. Edward Kastner (1878–1955). The nephew also named the *googolplex* (10 to the power googol), which to him meant a number one followed by so many zeroes that "your hand would get tired of writing before you finished."

Hyperbola: *See* Parabola.

Hypotenuse: Taken from the Greek words *hypo* and *teinein,* meaning "to stretch under." It was used by Greek mathematician Pythagoras (c. 540 B.C.) to describe the relationship of the legs of a right triangle to the longest side, or hypotenuse (*see* Figure 7). The Greek word is thought to be related to the Egyptian word *harpendopterai,* meaning "ropestretcher." In early Egypt a rope-stretcher was a man who reestablished boundary markers each spring after the Nile flood waters receded. This was done using the simplest right triangle with sides 3-4-5. Although the Egyptians clearly knew of this special case of the Pythagorean theorem, it is not clear whether they knew the general case of the theorem.

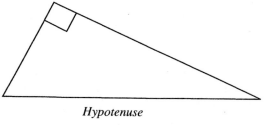

Hypotenuse

Figure 7

Hypothesis: Taken from the Greek words *hypo*, meaning "partial or incomplete" and *thenai*, meaning "put down." For the ancient Greeks, a hypothesis was a statement that was put down as a possible truth but had to be proved. It was incomplete until it was proven.

Inch: Taken from the Latin term *unicae*, meaning "twelfth part." In ancient Rome, the basic monetary unit was the *as*, a one-pound (Troy) copper coin. The *unicae* was $\frac{1}{12}$ the value of an *as*. An interesting sidelight to the derivation for inch is that the word *ounce* is also derived from the same Latin term. The length of an inch was established during the reign of King Edward II (1284–1327) of England when he declared an inch to be equal to "the length of three barleycorns, round and dry, taken from the middle of the ear, and laid end to end."

Integer: Taken from the Latin term *integer*, meaning "perfect, whole, complete." An integer is a number that is not fractional or irrational, but complete and whole.

Integral Calculus: Wilhelm Gottfried von Leibniz (1646–1716) and Johann Bernoulli (1667–1748) are said to have discussed the name for integral calculus, with Leibniz favoring *calculus sumatorius,* and Bernoulli preferring *calculus integralis*. In the end they compromised and used Bernoulli's term *calculus integralis,* but with Leibniz's symbol ∫ for integration. Actually, it was Johann Bernoulli's brother, Jacob Bernoulli (1654–1705), who first used the term *calculus integrali* in *Acta Eruditorium (1790).*

Interpolate: Taken from the Latin term *interpolare,* meaning "to adorn or furbish between." Interpolation is the process of determining, and thus adding, values between extremes.

Isosceles: Taken from the Greek words *iso* and *skelos,* meaning "equal legs," a description used today to identify triangles and trapezoids with at least two legs of equal length.

Knot: The term is derived from the ancient method of finding the speed of a ship at sea. A log of wood (from which comes the phrase "ship's log") was cast off the stern of the ship. Tied to the log was a rope which was knotted at regular intervals. As the ship moved away from the log, the rope was let out. The number of knots of rope let out during a specific time period determined the speed of the ship.

Line: Taken from the Latin term *linum,* meaning "flaxen chord." In ancient Rome flax was a prized product used to produce highly durable linen cloth and ropes. A flaxen cord was very sturdy and used for measuring lengths.

Logarithm: The term was first used by Scotsman John Napier in 1616 in his treatise that introduced logarithms. It is derived from the Greek terms *logos*, meaning "ratio," and *arithmos*, meaning "number." The shortened form of logarithm, "log," was first used in 1624 by Johann Kepler (1571–1630) in *Chilias Logarithmorum.*

Mantissa: This term, introduced by Henry Briggs (1561–1630) in 1624 in *Arithmetica Logarithmica,* is based on a Latin term *mantissa,* meaning "something added to a scale to meet a required value." In a logarithm, the mantissa is the portion after the decimal point, usually of minor value. Briggs also coined the term *characteristic* for the portion of a logarithm that precedes the decimal point. In his work, Briggs published his calculations of the logarithms for the numbers 1 to 20,000 and 90,000 to 100,000, each carried out to fourteen places!

Mathematics: Taken from the Greek term *mathematika*, which combines two words *manthanein*, meaning "to learn" and *mathema*, meaning "science."

Matrix: Taken from the Latin term *matrix,* meaning "pregnant animal." A matrix is an array of numbers with potential for problem-solving, much as a pregnant animal has potential for giving birth.

Mile: Taken from the Latin phrase *mille passus,* meaning "one thousand paces," a pace being the distance a soldier moved in two strides. A pace is a distance of about five feet, thus a thousand paces is about the distance of a standard mile.

Million: Taken from the Latin word *mille,* meaning "thousand." The word *million* literally means "great thousand," just as the word *salon (salle* plus *on)* means "great room." Some credit Marco Polo as the first user of the word million because he described the people he saw on his visit to Cathay as *millions persones,* or "many thousands." The word *million* first appeared in print in *Summa de Arithmetica,* a book published in 1494 by Italian mathematician Luca Paciola (1445–1514).

Minuend: Taken from the Latin term *numerus minuendus,* meaning "number to be diminished." *Subtrahend* is from the *numerus subtrahendus,* meaning "number to be subtracted."

Multiplication: Taken from the Latin *multi,* meaning "many" and plicare, meaning "fold." Thus the term *multiplication* means "replicating the number many times to obtain the solution."

Numerator: Taken from the Latin *numeros,* meaning "number." The term *denominator* is from the Latin term *denominare,* meaning "namer." The two terms which make up a fraction are thus named for their functions: The denominator names the fraction, and the numerator gives the number of parts of that fraction.

Obtuse: Taken from the Latin word *obtusus,* meaning "blunt." In contrast to an acute ("sharp") angle, an obtuse angle (*see* Figure 8) resembles a blunt point. In earlier times, a dull-witted person was considered obtuse.

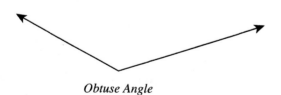

Obtuse Angle

Figure 8

Parabola: Taken from the Greek word *parabole,* meaning "to throw beside." In his great work, *Conic Sections,* Apollonius of Perga (262–190 b.c.) first used the words *parabola, hyperbola,* and *ellipse.* Apollonius derived the shapes of the circle, parabola, ellipse, and hyperbola from cross sections of a cone, hence his title, *Conic Sections.* A parabola is a curve that is beside or parallel to the boundary of the cone in which it is found. The term *ellipse is* derived from the Greek word *ellepsis,* meaning "to fall short, come up defective." In conic sections, the ellipse is short of the perfect shape, the circle. The term *hyperbola is* derived from the Greek words *hyper,* meaning "to throw," and *ballein,* meaning "beyond." A hyperbola is a curve that is thrown beyond the angle of a parabola. The plane that forms the hyperbola makes a larger angle than the plane that forms a parabola (*see* Figure 9).

It appears that these terms originated with the Pythagoreans, but Apollonius adopted them in *Conic Sections* to describe the relationships of curves formed when sections of a cone are taken. The standard equation for a parabola is $y^2 = px$; for an ellipse, $y^2 < px$; and for a hyperbola, $y^2 > px$. Note how the relationship of y^2 to px matches Apollonius' selection of Greek words to describe the respective curves.

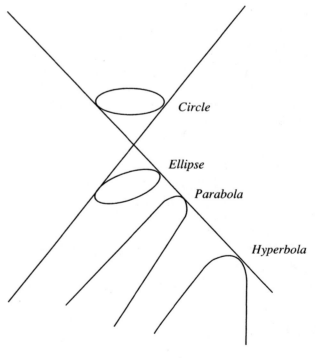

Circle

Ellipse

Parabola

Hyperbola

Figure 9

Parallel: Taken from the Greek word *parallelos,* meaning "beside one another."

Parentheses: Taken from the Greek term *parentithenai*, meaning "putting in beside." In an equation or a sentence, parentheses allow for putting numbers or words in beside other numbers or words.

Permutation: Taken from the Latin term *permutare*, meaning "to completely change." In mathematics, a permutation is a changing of the arrangements of members in a set.

Perpendicular: Taken from the Latin words *per*, meaning "thoroughly," and *pendre*, meaning "to hang." In ancient times, a perpendicular was derived by a hanging weight that was vertical to a horizontal surface.

Polar: The term, used to describe circular coordinates, was first used by Joseph Diez Gergonne (1771–1859). Gergonne is also known for Gergonne's point and for his work in projective geometry.

Polygon: Taken from the Greek term *polygonos*, meaning "using many angles." In contrast to the modern definition of *polygon*, "many sided," the original Greek term referred to the angles of the figure, not the sides.

Postulate: Taken from the Latin term *postulare*, meaning "to demand." A postulate is a statement of obvious fact, which demands acceptance. This is in contrast to a theorem, which must be sustained by a supporting argument.

Prism: Taken from the Greek word *prisma*, meaning "a thing sawed." A prism is a solid with faces formed by parallel planes, resembling an object that has been sawed by a craftsman.

Proportion: Taken from the Greek term *proportione*, meaning "for its own share." A proportionate amount is one which provides its own share.

Quotient: Taken from the Middle English word *quocient*, meaning "how many times." Division may be thought of as how many times one number is contained in another.

Radian: This relatively new term was coined by Professor James Thompson on a final exam he administered on June 5, 1873, at Queens College in Belfast, Ireland. The radian is an angle at the center of a circle which marks the boundaries of an arc in the circle equal in length to the radius.

Radical: Taken from the Arabic word *jidr*, meaning "plant-root." In Arabic mathematics texts, a square number was thought of as growing out of a root number (for example 49 growing out of 7). The process of determining that root from a square was somewhat more difficult than simpler calculations and so the root was extracted from the square, much as a plant with its root is extracted from the earth. The translation into Latin rendered *jidr* to *radix*, the Latin term for root. The term *square root* is a remnant of Arabic writings.

Radius: Taken from the Latin word *radius*, meaning "the spoke of a wheel." It was first used by French mathematician Peter Ramus (1515–1572) in his 1569 publication of *P. Rami Scholarium mathematicarvm kibri unus et triginti*.

Rhombus: Taken from the Greek word *rhombos*, meaning "magic wheel." A rhombus placed vertically on one of its acute angles is similar to a top or magic wheel used for divination by ancient Greeks.

Rod: Taken from the Middle English word *rodd*. As with other measurements, the rod was not standardized at first. As late as 1536, Jacob Koble gave the following definition for a rod: "To find the length of a measuring rod the right way, and as it is common in the craft … take sixteen men, short men and tall ones, as they leave church and let each one of them put one shoe after the other and the length thus obtained shall be a just and common measuring rod to survey the land with."

Scalene: Taken from the Greek word *scalenos*, meaning "uneven." A scalene is a triangle of uneven or unequal sides.

Secant: Taken from the Latin word *secans*, meaning "cutting line." A secant is a line that cuts through a circle (*see* Figure 10).

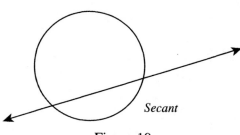

Secant

Figure 10

Segment: Taken from the Latin term *secare*, meaning "to cut." A segment is a portion cut from a line. The word *sector* is also derived from the same Latin term.

Sin, Tan, Sec: These abbreviations of trigonometric functions were all devised by Albert Girard (c. 1590–c. 1633). He is best known for his work with complex numbers.

Sine: The word for the trigonometric sine function has a complex history. The first use of a term for what we call the sine function was by Hindu mathematician Aryabhata, who wrote mathematics texts around the year 500. He called the sine function *ardhajya*, meaning "half-chord" (*see* Figure 11). This was subsequently shortened to *jya*. Arab mathematicians in turn translated this term to *jiba* in their texts.

In 1085 Christian forces in Spain recovered the Moorish city of Toledo, a great Arabic learning center. Many Western European scholars flocked there to translate the Arabic works into Latin, among them a scholar named Gerard of Cremona (1114-1187). Among the works he translated were Ptolemy's *Algamest*, Euclid's *Elements*, Archimedes' *Measurement of a Circle*, Apollonius' *Conic Sections*, and al-Khwarizmi's algebra texts. Gerard is said to have been the most prolific translator of Arabic texts in history. Among his translations is the Latin word for sine. The Arabic word for sine, *jiba*, was written with no vowels, simply as *jb*, and Gerard translated it as *jaib*, which means "bay, cove, or fold." The Latin translation of *jaib* is sinus, which became the modern word *sine*. The related term cosine was first used in 1620 by Edmund Gunther

(1581–1626) in his book *Canon Triangulorum*. Gunther was also the inventor of the basic slide rule.

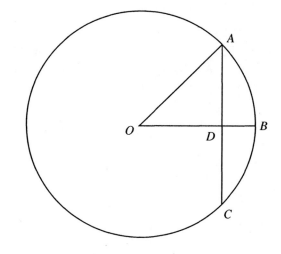

If circle O *has radius* 0A=1, *then the sine of* ∠AOB=AD/OA=AD/1=AD. AD *is one half of chord* AC

Figure 11

Skew: Taken from the Middle English word *skiuh-wan*, meaning "to escape." Skew lines are in two different planes. One of the lines has escaped the plane which contains the other line.

Subtraction: Taken from the Latin words *sub* and *trahere*, meaning "below" and "draw out," respectively. Subtraction is the drawing out of one number from another.

Subtrahend: *See* Minuend.

Surd: Taken from the Latin word *surdus*, in turn translated from the Arabic word *jadhr*, meaning "deaf root." The Arabic word was taken from the Greek *alogos*, meaning "speechless." In both Greek and Arabic the value of a surd representing a sum such as $\sqrt{3} + \sqrt{5}$ was impossible to determine, since the individual values are irrational. Such a value was thus speechless, or a deaf root (*see* Radical).

Tangent: Taken from the Latin term *tangere,* meaning "to touch." A tangent line is a line that touches a circle at one point. The term was first used for the trigonometric function in 1583 by the obscure British mathematician Thomas Finck (1561–1646) in *Geometria routundi.* In a circle of radius 1, the tangent of the central angle is equal to the length of the tangent segment which forms the central angle (*see* Figure 12).

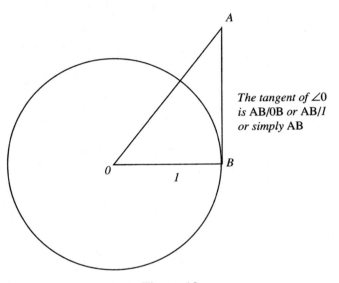

The tangent of ∠0 is AB/0B or AB/1 or simply AB

Figure 12

Tessellation: Taken from the Latin word *tesserea,* a term that described the small square tiles used for Roman mosaics, such as those found today in Ravenna, Italy. In a tessellation, geometric figures tile a plane leaving no empty spaces, much like a mosaic tiling.

Theorem: Taken from the Greek word *theoros,* meaning "spectacle, to look at." For the ancient Greeks, theorems were statements to be observed as laws, with a proof worthy of observation.

Thousand: Taken from the Gothic term *thus-hundi,* meaning "swollen hundred."

Trapezoid: Taken from the Greek word *trapeza,* meaning "table." Trapezoid-shaped tables are still common today.

Vector: Taken from the Latin term *vectus,* meaning "to carry." A vector carries a force along its directional heading. The word *vector* was first used by Irish mathematician Sir William Rowan Hamilton (1805–1865) in 1845.

Yard: Taken from the Old English word *gerd,* meaning "staff or rod." The measurement for a yard was originally established by King Henry I (1069–1135) of England as the distance from the tip of of the king's outstretched hand to the tip of his royal nose, similar to King Charlemagne of France's suggestion in 799 that the king's foot be the standard unit of length. Naturally, the length varied according to the stature of the king. The length was finally settled by King Henry VII (1547-1585) of England as three feet, and was so inscribed on a bronze bar.

Zero: The word *zero* has a long history. The concept of zero began with the Chinese, who as early as the fourth century B.C. represented zero as a blank space on a counting board. By the third century A.D., Hindu mathematicians were using a heavy dot to mark its place in calculations. The dot was eventually replaced by an empty circle. The oldest surviving use of an empty circle for zero is on a temple inscription in Gvalior, India, and dates from 840. There are also claims that the zero symbol appeared in inscriptions in Cambodia and Sumatra as early as 683, which supports arguments that the zero symbol was invented in China.

The Hindu word for zero was *sunya,* meaning "empty." This was transliterated into Arabic as *as-sifr,* with the similar meaning "vacant." This was, in turn, translated into Latin as *zephyrum.* Later renditions of the term varied such as *zepiro, zeuero,* and *zéro.* The concept of zero and the use of Hindu-Arabic numerals were resisted by Western European merchants. The first European mathematician to strongly advocate the use of zero was Leonardo of Pisa (1180–1250), better known as Fibonacci, who used the term *zephirum* in his book *Liber Abaci.* As late as 1298, however, the City Council of Florence, Italy, outlawed any system but Roman numerals, claiming that the Arabic numerals were too easy to falsify, since "one can with ease make one out of another such as turning the zero into a six or a nine."

160

6

Solutions and Extensions

1: Magic Squares

Solutions

There are 808 different possible arrangements for a 4 × 4 magic square. Have students share alternative arrangements they discover.

8	1	6
3	5	7
4	9	2

16	3	2	13
5	10	11	8
9	6	7	12
4	15	14	1

Extension

Students will likely find solutions to the 3 × 3 magic square that at first glance may appear to be different from the one given. Correct arrangements must be flips or rotations of the unique solution shown above. This presents an opportunity to discuss transformations with the students.

2: The Möbius Band

Solutions

1. A Möbius band has only one side. The line will appear on every portion of the band.
2. The result is one large Möbius band.
3. This time the result is a large, thin Möbius band and a smaller, wider Möbius band that are interlinked.

There is a story about Möbius and his discovery of the Möbius band. While on vacation in a small cabin in the wilderness, he was pestered by insects in his bedroom. He fashioned a flycatcher by affixing some sticky substance to a strip of paper that he hung above the bed. He looped the ends of the paper together, giving one end a half-twist before attaching the ends to prevent the loop from collapsing on itself. His flycatcher worked quite well. One morning, while resting in bed, Möbius looked admiringly at his flycatcher and noticed it had only one side and one edge! This was the beginning of the Möbius band and his study of topology.

There have been a number of technical applications of the Möbius band. Belts driving machinery have been designed in the shape of a Möbius band so that the belt will wear uniformly rather than wearing out on a single side as in a conventional belt.

Extension

Have students explore what happens when the result from exercise 2 is cut down the middle again. (The result is two double-twisted bands that are interlinked in two places.)

3: Star Polygons

Solution

Poinsot was not the first to explore star polygons. They are first described by Thomas Bradwardine (1290–1349) who later became Archbishop of Canterbury but died of the plague after serving only a few months in office.

There are many other star polygon patterns. The pattern (5,2) produces the familiar five-point star. Another star polygon pattern is (9,2). Students could draw these and be encouraged to find others. The patterns may be colored to enhance their beauty.

Extension

The pattern (8,5) is the same as (8,3). Ask students to determine why. These polygons can be used to introduce modular counting systems.

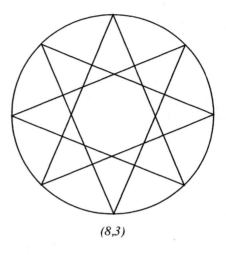

(8,3)

4: Boole Cards

Solution

The resulting curve is a parabola. Changing the angle of the rays or the spacing of the points will distort the parabola by making its curve more or less extreme.

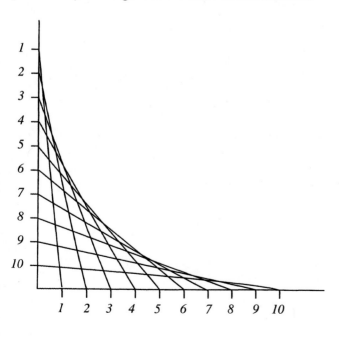

Mary Everest Boole was raised in France under the influence of her father, who was a great believer in homeopathy. (Her uncle was George Everest of Mt. Everest fame.) Daily ice baths followed by brisk walks were part of the family's routine. Mary Boole survived this regimen and at age twenty-three married George Boole, an Irish mathematician known for his new algebra, a forerunner to the logic used in today's computer programming.

At thirty-two, Mary Everest Boole was a widow with five children. She obtained a job as the librarian of Queen's College in London. Her Boole cards, begun as a "recreation for nervous invalids," soon progressed to "a thing which woman can manage without agitation or public discussion." It is clear that Boole was sensitive to the prevailing negative attitude concerning the ability of women to follow intellectual pursuits. Perhaps she hoped the Boole cards would provide some mental stimulation for women of her time. A collection of her activities were published in 1906 by family friend Edith Somerville in *A Rhythmic Approach to Mathematics*.

5: The Wolf, the Goat, and the Cabbage

Solution

Let W represent the wolf, C represent the cabbage, G represent the goat, F represent the ferryman, and I represent the river.

1. Ferry the goat across the river to the west bank. $G\ F\ I\ W, C$
2. Return to the east bank. $G\ I\ W, C, F$
3. Take the wolf across the river. $G, W, F\ I\ C$
4. Return to the east bank with the goat. $W\ I\ G, C, F$
5. Leave the goat on the east bank and take the cabbage across to the west bank. $W, C, F\ I\ G$
6. Return to the east bank. $W, C\ I\ G, F$
7. Take the goat across to the west bank. $W, C, G, F\ I$

Extension

This might be a more interesting problem if students have to act out the solution with small groups, assuming roles of wolf, goat, cabbage, and ferryman. A second solution is to bring the cabbage across the river in step 3 and the wolf in step 5.

6: The Sieve of Eratosthenes

Solution

The prime numbers are 2, 3, 5, 7, 11, 13, 17, 19, and 23.

Extension

Students could use Eratosthenes' sieve to find all the prime numbers up to 100.

7: Lewis Carroll's Doublets

Solutions

1. CAT-COT-DOT-DOG
2. CAR-CAT-MAT-MET-JET
3. COOL-FOOL-FOOT-BOOT-BOLT-BELT

With the publication of *Alice in Wonderland,* everything changed for Lewis Carroll. He was famous throughout the continent of Europe, and everything else he published, including recreational mathematics, found a ready audience. Some of his recreational mathematics deal with logic problems and word puzzles, such as his doublets. The problems were frequently published in magazines with prizes given to the best answers submitted by readers. First prize for the doublets problems was a first edition proof of the March 29, 1879, issue of *Vanity Fair* which contained the first doublets.

8: Needle in a π Stack

Solution

As a matter of fact, the exact value of π will result with an infinite number of tosses. Thus, class totals will give a closer approximation of π than will the results of just one student.

Not all of Buffon's mathematical ideas were accepted. He unsuccessfully proposed a base-12 system for the French measurement system; the decimal system was used when the metric system was established shortly after his death.

Extension

The results of the experiment may be used to introduce the concept of infinite trials in probability theory.

9: The Inventor of Chess

Solutions

Square 20 = $5242.88

Square 30 = $5,368,709.12

If the king had filled the board, the number of grains of wheat on square 64 alone would be more than 9,223,372,037,000,000,000, a considerable amount for even a king to pay. The total number of grains of wheat on the entire board would be an amount that would cover the surface of the entire earth to a depth of one inch! The conclusion of the story is that Sissa did not expect such a payment but sought to teach his monarch a lesson in mathematics.

10: The Fibonacci Sequence

Solution

The resulting pattern (1, 1, 2, 3, 5, 8, 13, 21, 34, 55, 89, 144) is known as the Fibonacci sequence. In the Fibonacci sequence, each number is the sum of the two previous numbers. The ratio of any number to the next number converges on the approximate value of .618. This value is called the golden ratio, and has been shown to be the most aesthetically pleasing proportion for the sides of a rectangle. Rectangles whose sides have this ratio are called golden rectangles and are incorporated in great art works, architecture, and in commercially produced products such as posters, postcards, and cereal boxes.

Month	Pairs of Babies	Pairs of Adults	Total Pairs
Jan. 1	0	1	1
Feb. 1	1	1	2
Mar. 1	1	2	3
Apr. 1	2	3	5
May 1	3	5	8
Jun. 1	5	8	13
Jul. 1	8	13	21
Aug. 1	13	21	34
Sep. 1	21	34	55
Oct. 1	34	55	89
Nov. 1	55	89	144
Dec. 1	89	144	233
Jan 1.	144	233	377

11: As I Was Going to St. Ives

Solution

It's a trick question. Actually, only one person was going *to* St. Ives. That person met an unusual party of 2,801 (1 man, 7 wives, 49 sacks, 343 cats, and 2,401 kittens) coming *from* the direction of St. Ives.

Extension

There is another version of this rhyme in Fibonacci's *Liber Abaci* (1202):

> There are seven old women on the road to Rome.
> Each woman has seven mules;
> Each mule carries seven sacks;
> Each sack contains seven loaves;
> With each loaf are seven knives;
> And each knife is in seven sheaths.
> Women, mules, sacks, loaves, knives and sheaths;
> How many in all are there on the road to Rome?

In this case each successive description is a power of seven: 7 women, 49 mules, 343 sacks, 2401 loaves, 16,807 knives, and 117,648 sheaths. This version of the problem allows for a discussion of exponents.

12: "There It Lies"

Solution

Gauss paired the numbers from 1 to 100 as follows:

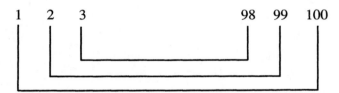

He discovered that each pair totaled 101. There are fifty such pairs from 1 to 100, so the sum is equal to 50 • 101, or 5050.

Extension

There is a general formula for summing consecutive numbers from 1 to any number *n*:

$$\frac{n}{2}(n + 1), \text{ or } \frac{100}{2}(101).$$

When *n* is 100, then $\frac{100}{2}(101) = 50 \cdot 101 = 5{,}050$, the same answer Gauss determined with his method. Students might benefit from exploring other summation formulas, such as a formula for the sum of odd integers.

13: The Circumference of the Earth

Solution

Eratosthenes used the following givens to determine the earth's circumference:

- The earth is round, having a total of 360 degrees.
- When the sun was directly above Syene, the sun's rays cast a shadow at a $\frac{1}{12}$) degree angle.
- The distance from Syene to Alexandria was 5000 stadia.

Eratosthenes set up the following equation to determine the earth's circumference:

Let x represent the circumference of the earth.

$$\frac{7\frac{1}{12}°}{360°} = \frac{5000 \text{ stadia}}{x}$$

$x = (360 \cdot 5{,}000) \div 7.083$

$360 \cdot 5000 = 1{,}800{,}000$

$1{,}800{,}000 \div 7.083 = 254{,}129.6061$

$x = 254{,}129.6061$ stadias $= 127{,}064{,}803$ feet

$= 24{,}065.30361$ miles

Using these figures, the earth's circumference works out to be about 24,065 miles, within 900 miles of the actual figure.

Eratosthenes was known as the "All-Around One" because he excelled in so many areas besides mathematics. In old age he suffered from progressive ophthalmia. Rather than spend his last days as a blind man, he starved himself to death.

Extension

Geometry students may be asked to determine the role of parallel lines in Eratosthenes calculations.

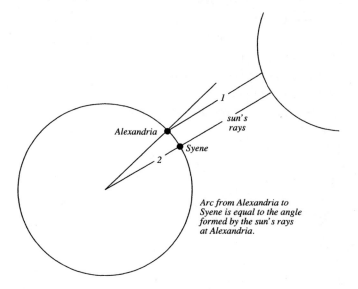

Arc from Alexandria to Syene is equal to the angle formed by the sun's rays at Alexandria.

Since the sun's rays are parallel, angle 1, which Eratosthenes measured in Alexandria, must be equal to angle 2. Thus, the arc measure between Alexandria and Syene must also equal $\angle 2$, or $7\frac{1}{12}$ degrees. With this information Eratosthenes could then set up the proportion shown above.

14: The Formulas of Heron and Brahmagupta

Solutions

The area of the triangle is about 54. The area of the cyclic quadrilateral is about 66.

Heron is also known for his writings on algebra and geometry, and for his primitive steam engine. Bhaskara was one of the first mathematicians to write about signed integers.

15: Al-Khwarizmi's Will

Solution

Al-Khwarizmi clearly wanted a son to inherit twice as much as his wife. He also wanted his wife to inherit twice as much as a daughter. Let x represent the wife's share. The following equation could be used to distribute al-Khwarizmi's estate: $2x + x + \frac{1}{2}x = 1$. The son would receive $\frac{4}{7}$, the wife $\frac{2}{7}$, and the daughter $\frac{1}{7}$, thus maintaining the relative portions of the inheritance as specified by al-Khwarizmi in his will.

16: The Life of Diophantus

Solution

Let *n* represent the number of years which Diophantus lived.

$$(\tfrac{1}{6})n + (\tfrac{1}{12})n + (\tfrac{1}{7})n + 5 + (\tfrac{1}{2})n + 4 = n$$

$$n = 84$$

Most of what is known about Diophantus' works comes to us from commentaries by Hypatia (c. 400) about 150 years later and from Arab mathematicians. Of the thirteen books which formed his *Arithmetica*, only six survive, along with a small fragment of his tract *On Polygonal Numbers*. Translations of these works were discovered in the writings of later Arab mathematicians.

17: America's Greatest Puzzlers

Solution

The string is 65,536 inches (approximately 5460 feet) long. If the ball is unwound to a single strand of string, the string would be in the shape of one very long cylinder that has the same volume as it did when it was in the shape of a sphere. In this case the volume of the sphere, $\frac{4}{3}\pi r^3$, equals the volume of the cylinder, $\pi r^2 h$. (h stands for the height of the cylinder, or in this case, the length of the string).

$$\tfrac{4}{3}\pi r^3 = \pi r^2 h.$$
$$\tfrac{4}{3}\pi (12)(12)(12) = \pi \tfrac{3}{16} \cdot \tfrac{3}{16}(h)$$

As the books are arranged, the front cover of Volume 1 is on the right side of Volume 1 and the back cover of Volume 10 is on the left side of Volume 10. The worm does not move through either Volume 1 or Volume 10. So, the worm would travel 16 inches.

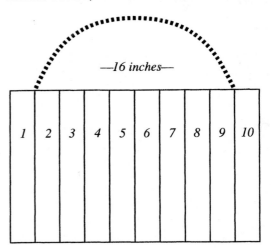

—16 inches—

| 1 | 2 | 3 | 4 | 5 | 6 | 7 | 8 | 9 | 10 |

18: Euler's Formula

Solution

Euler found that for all polyhedra $V + F - E = 2$. A further challenge for students is to imagine drilling any polygon-shaped hole through a polyhedron to discover if Euler's formula is still true. (It is.)

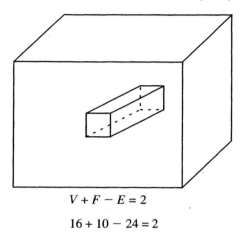

$$V + F - E = 2$$

$$16 + 10 - 24 = 2$$

Extension

Euler also found an interesting formula for the volume of a triangular pyramid such as in the figure below. If the six edges are lettered a, b, c, d, e, and f, then the volume formula is:

$$V = \tfrac{1}{12}(4a^2b^2d^2 - a^2(b^2 + d^2 + e^2)^2 - b^2(a^2 + d^2 - f^2)^2 - d^2(d^2 + b^2 - c^2) + (b^2 - d^2 + e^2)(a^2 + b^2 - f^2)(a^2 + b^2 - c^2))$$

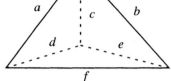

19: *Pons Asinorum*

Solution

Prove triangle *DCA* congruent to triangle *FBA* by "side-angle-side," then use corresponding parts of congruent triangles to prove that angle *ABC* equals angle *ACB*.

In the Middle Ages, monastic schools were essentially the only institutions of learning in Western Europe. The courses of study included the *trivium* (grammar, rhetoric, and dialectic) and the *quadrivium* (arithmetic, geometry, astronomy, and music). Much of the mathematics curriculum of the quadrivium was established by Boethius (475–524), who was later a martyr for his Christian faith. Roger Bacon (1220–1292) gave Proposition 5 the name *Elefuga*, which he said meant "the flight of the miserable ones" from mathematics.

Extension

The proof is much easier if an auxiliary line such as an altitude from point *A* is drawn. Such lines violated Euclid's sense of what is properly an auxiliary line and so were not allowed in the proof of Proposition 5. Students may wish to try a proof with an altitude or a similar auxiliary line.

20: Branchion's Claim to Fame

Solution

Branchion did no original work in mathematics except this theorem and related conclusions. One cannot help but wonder if his early success led to a life of unfulfilled expectations.

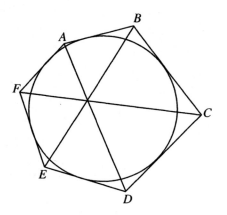

Extension

When he was only sixteen, Blaise Pascal (1623–1662) made a discovery along the same lines as Branchion. Pascal wrote a one-page paper entitled *Essay on Conics,* which contained his theorem of the mystic hexagram. The theorem stated: *If a hexagon with no parallel sides is inscribed in a conic section, then the three intersection points of the three pairs of opposite sides will be collinear.*

Students may wish to try this construction. Caution them to avoid drawing a hexagon whose opposite sides are close to parallel, since the resulting intersection point is likely to be off the page.

21: The Shortest Proof in Geometry

Solution

If the four triangles and the square are arranged as shown below, they form two squares, an *a*-square (the shaded area) and a *b*-square from the original larger *c*-square.

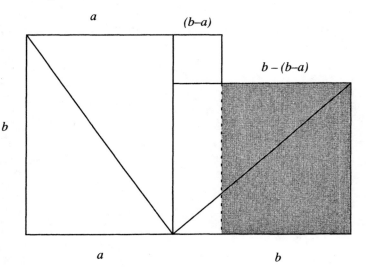

Extension

There are literally hundreds of proofs of the Pythagorean theorem. One of the more interesting was discovered by James Garfield (1831–1881), five years before he became president of the United States. In the following figure, the area of the trapezoid is equal to the sum of areas of the three triangles.

$$(a + b) \left(\tfrac{1}{2}\right)(a + b) = \tfrac{1}{2}(ab) + \tfrac{1}{2}(ab) + \tfrac{1}{2}(c^2).$$
$$a^2 + 2ab + b^2 = 2ab + c^2$$
$$a^2 + b^2 = c^2$$

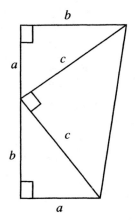

22: The Simson Line

Solution

If correctly constructed, the three points *X*, *Y*, and *Z* are always collinear.

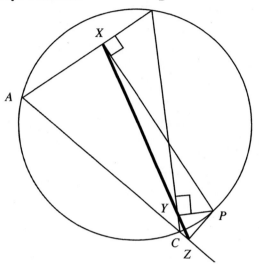

How did Simson's name get attached to Wallace's theorem? Simson was well known for his eighteenth-century English translation and commentary of Euclid's *Elements*. His book was so popular it was still being used in mid-nineteenth-century England and had twenty-four printings in England alone. In later commentaries, when Wallace's theorem was included along with Simson's translation of Euclid, the theorem became associated with Simson, not Wallace.

Some have blamed Simson's book for the fact that British mathematicians were slow to develop analytical methods to deal with analysis problems. It seems that Simson's geometry had created a mind set among budding mathematicians for the synthetic geometry of the Greeks and not for the analytical methods of Descartes and others.

23: The Nine-Point Circle

Solution

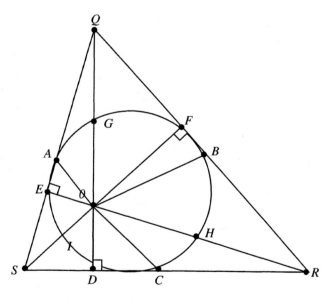

Feurbach died at a young age as a result of being imprisoned. He was arrested one day without warning along with nineteen other graduate students for belonging to a subversive organization when an undergraduate. During his fourteen months of incarceration he attempted suicide several times, but eventually he was released and exonerated. The stay in prison left its mark, however, and he was never the same. He began to teach again but suffered a breakdown. He recovered to teach yet again but one day brought a sword to class and threatened to run through any student who did not perform well at the blackboard! That marked the end of his teaching career. He then began a slow decent into madness which ended when he died six years later in 1834.

Extension

Leonard Euler (1701–1783) discovered Euler's line in the constructions of certain points in an triangle. Euler's line joins the orthocenter, the circumcenter, and the centroid. Students could verify by construction that the midpoint of Euler's line (actually Euler's segment, in this case) is also the center of the nine-point circle.

24: Fermat's Point

Solution

The practical application of Fermat's point may be highlighted by selecting actual towns in the locale. Have students determine by construction the ideal location of a central office for a fictitious company. (Naturally, this method ignores other factors impacting on the ideal location of a central office, such as proximity to a highway, and location of business centers.)

Extension

Some sources suggest Fermat posed the question of minimum distance to Evangelista Torricelli (1608–1647). Torricelli found the same point but by a slightly different construction. Using the same three equilateral triangles as constructed for discovering Fermat's point, draw circumcircles (circumscribed circles) about each one of them. The circumcircles will intersect in the same minimum distance point. Have students reproduce Torricelli's construction and label the result Torricelli's point in his honor.

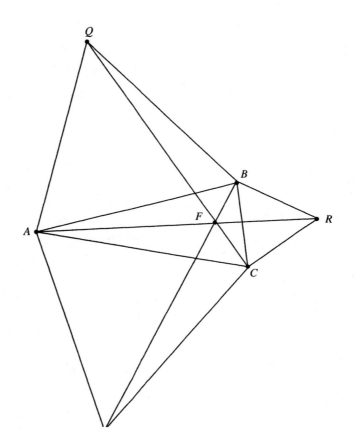

Bibliography

Baron, M. *The Origins of the Infinitesimal Calculus*. New York: Dover Publications, Inc., 1969.

Bell, T.E. *Men in Mathematics*. New York: Simon and Schuster, 1937.

Bergamini, David. *Mathematics*. Alexandria, Va.: Time-Life Books, 1970.

Berggren, J. *Episodes in the Mathematics of Medieval Islam*. New York: Springer-Verlag, 1986.

Boyer, Carl B. *The History of Mathematics*. New York: John Wiley & Sons, Inc., 1968.

———. *The History of the Calculus and Its Conceptual Development*. New York: Dover Publications, Inc., 1949.

Bunt, Lucas N., et al. *The Historical Roots of Elementary Mathematics*. New York: Dover Publications, Inc., 1976.

Burton, David M. *The History of Mathematics: An Introduction*. Boston: Allyn and Bacon, 1985.

Cajori, Florian. *A History of Mathematical Notation*. Chicago: Open Court, 1928.

Dunham, William. *Journey Through Genius—The Great Theorems of Mathematics*. New York: John Wiley & Sons, Inc., 1990.

Eves, Howard W. *In Mathematical Circles*. Boston: Prindle, Weber, & Smith, 1969.

———. *Mathematical Circles Revisited*. Boston: Prindle, Weber, & Smith, 1971.

———. *Mathematical Circles Squared*. Boston: Prindle, Weber, & Smith, 1972.

———. *Mathematical Circles Adieu*. Boston: Prindle, Weber, & Smith, 1977.

———. *Return to Mathematical Circles*. Boston: Prindle, Weber, & Smith, 1982.

———. *An Introduction to the History of Mathematics*. Philadelphia: Saunders College, 1983.

———. *Great Moments in Mathematics Before 1650*. Washington, D.C.: Mathematical Association of America, 1983.

———. *Great Moments in Mathematics After 1650*. Washington, D.C.: Mathematical Association of America, 1983.

Fauvel, John, and Jeremy Gray, eds. *The History of Mathematics—A Reader*. London: Macmillan Press, 1987.

Heath, Thomas L. *A History of Greek Mathematics, Volumes I and II*. New York: Dover Publications, 1981.

Hoffman, P. *Archimedes Revenge*. New York: W.W. Norton & Co., 1988.

Hofstadter, Douglas R. *Godel, Escher and Bach: An Eternal Golden Braid*. New York: Vintage Books, 1979.

Hollingsdale, S. *Makers of Mathematics*. London: Penguin Books, 1989.

Huntley, H.E. *The Divine Proposition*. New York: Dover Publications, Inc., 1970.

Jacobs, H. *Mathematics: A Human Endeavor*. San Francisco: W.H. Freeman, 1981.

Kline, M. *Mathematical Thought from Ancient to Modern Times*. New York: Oxford University Press, 1972.

Kline, M. *Mathematics in Western Culture*. New York: Dover Publications, Inc., 1964.

McGinty, H., et al. "A Brief Historical Dictionary of Mathematical Terms." *The Mathematics Teacher* 78(8).

National Council of Teachers of Mathematics. *Geometry in the Mathematics Curriculum (31st Yearbook)*. Reston, Va.: National Council of Teachers of Mathematics, 1973.

———. *Historical Topics for Mathematics Classroom*. Washington, D.C.: National Council of Teachers of Mathematics, 1969.

Osen, Lynn M. *Women in Mathematics*. Cambridge, Mass.: MIT Press, 1974.

Pappas. Theoni. *The Joy of Mathematics*. San Carlos, Calif.: Wide World Publications, 1986.

———. *More Joy of Mathematics*. San Carlos, Calif.: Wide World Publications, 1991.

Sommons, G. *Calculus Gems—Brief Lives and Memorable Mathematics*. New York: McGraw-Hill, 1992.

Struik, D. *A Source Book in Mathematics 1200–1800*. Princeton: Princeton Univ. Press, 1969.

Swetz. F. And Kao. T. *Was Pythagoras Chinese?* Harrisburg, Pa.: Penn State University Press, 1978.

Zeintarn, M. *A History of Computing*. Framingham, Mass.: C.W. Communications, 1981.